# PUZZLES
# TO UNWIND

Published in 2020 by Welbeck
An imprint of Welbeck Non-Fiction Limited,
part of Welbeck Publishing Group
20 Mortimer Street
London W1T 3JW

10 9 8 7 6 5 4 3 2 1

A CIP catalogue for this book is available from the
British Library.

ISBN 978-1-78739-208-3

Printed in the United Kingdom

Content previously published as *Classic Puzzles*

# PUZZLES TO UNWIND

**CLASSIC PUZZLES TO HELP CALM YOUR MIND**

# INTRODUCTION

The modern world is mentally more demanding than ever before. With screens now ever-present, it is becoming more and more difficult to switch off from the frantic 21st century world and relax.

In *Puzzles to Unwind* you will be challenged by a number of classic puzzles, such as crosswords, arrowords and keywords, as well as a series of variations on these traditional puzzles. Each is designed to provide a stern challenge, and the different approaches you will need to take to solve each of them should test all aspects of your mental faculties – as well as providing much enjoyment!

Make a cup of tea, settle down and let the worries of the world fall from your shoulders as you get stuck in to the many problems and posers before you.

# ROUNDABOUT

Solutions to Radial clues (1 to 24) either start from the outer edge of the circle and read inwards, or start from the inner ring and read outwards to the edge (so they are all five-letter words). Solutions to Circular clues read in either a clockwise or an anticlockwise direction around the circle.

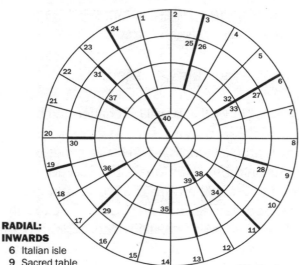

**RADIAL:**

**INWARDS**
6 Italian isle
9 Sacred table
10 Show-off
11 One who stares
17 Perspiration
19 Clever
20 Rush
21 Mountain ridge

14 Separate
15 Horrify
16 Savour
18 Stand a round
22 Consumer
23 Dog-___, well-worn
24 Baby carriages

**OUTWARDS**
1 Three of a kind (in cards)
2 Trivial
3 Irritating
4 Country of Asia
5 Inappropriate
7 Gaelic nationality
8 Hunting dog (archaic)
12 Stage whisper
13 Trembling poplar

**CIRCULAR:**
**CLOCKWISE**
6 Inexpensive
11 Mildest
19 Fragment of pottery
24 Cunning
26 Sleep (colloq)
27 Fire remains

28 Burden
33 Early Scotsmen
34 Fastener
35 Church recess
36 Comfort
37 Characteristic
39 Ancient Greek city state
40 Buccaneer

**ANTICLOCKWISE**
5 Scottish river
25 Domesticated
29 Vetch
30 Ruminant's stomach
31 Period of time
32 Commercials
38 Employee

*See answer 198*

# MISSING LINKS

The answer to each clue is a word which has a link with each of the three words listed. This word may come at the end (eg Head linked with Beach, Big and Hammer), at the beginning (eg Black linked with Beauty, Board and Jack) or a mixture of the two (eg Stone linked with Hail, Lime and Wall).

## ACROSS

1 Basket, Lunch, Table (6)
4 Head, Inspection, Sand (3)
7 Cue, Mobile, Pilot (4)
8 Money, Police, Racket (10)
9 Cobra, Penguin, Prawn (4)
10 Ant, Foot, Toy (7)
14 Master, Ring, Word (3)
15 Bank, Count, Whale (5)
17 Drip, Run, Spell (3)
18 Camera, Coffee, Replay (7)
23 Health, Junk, Processor (4)
25 Official, Prior, Ring (10)
26 Bamboo, Raspberry, Sugar (4)
27 Domestic, Name, Shop (3)
28 Dryer, Up, Woman (6)

## DOWN

1 Hanger, Rice, Round (5)
2 Country, Examine, Section (5)
3 Home, Man, World (5)
4 Fund, Star, Winner (5)
5 Petrol, Think, Top (4)
6 High, Issue, Lamp (8)
11 Lucky, Sherbet, Stick (3)
12 Baba, Punch, Truffle (3)
13 Column, Gain, Touch (8)
15 Jump, Lift, Slope (3)
16 Desert, Poison, Race (3)
19 Hen, Owl, Stag (5)
20 Indoor, Political, Stage (5)
21 Back, Eye, False (5)
22 Biscuit, Mark, Running (5)
24 Down, End, Skin (4)

*See answer 198*

# SKELETON CROSSWORD

Have double the fun with this puzzle: you've got to fill in the answers and the black squares! We've given you the bare bones to start and it will help you to know that the black squares in the finished grid form a symmetrical pattern, so that every black square has at least one other corresponding black square.

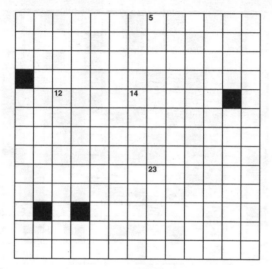

**ACROSS**

1 Made uneven
8 Smaller quantity
9 Increase
10 List of options
13 Bind up (an injury)
16 Thick mass or tuft
17 Evocative of a past style
18 Dark area
19 Bid in advance
20 Labourer
21 Polished
24 Bunch of flowers
27 Anxiety, disturbance
28 Corner
29 Burning slightly

**DOWN**

2 Owned by us
3 Rubberneck
4 Number in a rowing team
5 Minor actor
6 Flawed
7 Fictitious name
11 Go with
12 Colouring spread over a surface
13 Rider's heel spikes
14 Jewish religious leader
15 Caper
22 Reasoned judgment
23 Supply food
25 Skin irritation
26 Godsend

*See answer 198*

# JIG-WORD

No clues – just pattern and answers – but can you fit them in?

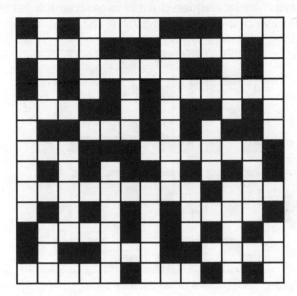

| 3-letter words | DAIS | ONION |
|---|---|---|
| AIM | DOGE | TEMPO |
| CAN | EARN | |
| CRY | FARM | **6-letter words** |
| MUM | LATE | ENFOLD |
| NOD | PLAN | INFANT |
| NOW | TARN | KARATE |
| OAR | VERA | NONAGE |
| RED | | RANDOM |
| SET | **5-letter words** | |
| TOM | CREAK | **8-letter word** |
| TWO | DREAR | PRETENCE |
| | IDIOM | |
| **4-letter words** | IMAGE | **9-letter word** |
| AREA | INFER | GRENADIER |

See answer 198

# DILEMMA

Two straightforward crosswords – but their clues have been mixed up. You have to decide which clue belongs to which pattern, but two words have been entered to give you a start.

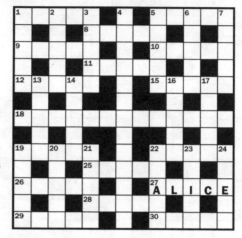

**ACROSS**

1 Play a guitar
5 Barred enclosures
8 Group of singers
9 Greek epic written by Homer
10 Diminish
11 Leg joint
12 Hard outer-covering
15 Canoe
18 Young relations
19 Improbable comedy
22 Perspire
25 Claude ___, French impressionist painter
26 Film award
27 Heavenly messenger
28 Northern city
29 Passenger ship
30 Fashion

1 Annoyed
5 Belt
8 White heron
9 Pit worker
10 Enthusiastic
11 Savoury jelly
12 Inexpensive
15 Door fastener
18 Spiral slide (6-7)
19 Love, worship
22 Salad plant
25 Showery month
26 Goddess of hunting
27 Wonderland girl
28 Bury
29 Coarse string
30 Part of a flower

## DOWN

1 Child's magazine
2 Lift up
3 Fight
4 Kind, merciful
5 Strong metal
6 Meat juice
7 Dehydrate
13 Biblical king
14 Holiday ship
16 Give permission
17 Board-game
19 Distant, supercilious
20 Quantities of paper
21 Ahead of time
22 Hold tightly
23 Bird of prey
24 Incantation

1 ___ roll, cylindrical sponge
2 Sixteenth of a pound
3 Bravery award
4 Crushed with grief (6-7)
5 Fissure
6 Correct
7 Smooth, glossy
13 'Laughing' animal
14 Loft
16 Tree of the birch family
17 Centre of an amphitheatre
19 Becomes less colourful
20 Happen
21 Electronic communication (1-4)
22 Begin
23 Proclamation
24 Covered with slabs of baked clay

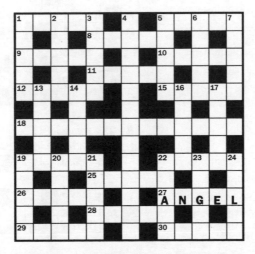

11

*See answer 198*

# PIECEWORD

With the help of the Across clues only, can you fit the 35 pieces into their correct positions in the empty grid (which, when completed, will exhibit a symmetrical pattern)?

## ACROSS

1. Mock; secret hoard
2. Wicked; of the moon; Sicily's volcano
3. False; tranquillity
4. Pivot; colossus; horse's pace
5. On the flat; male fowl
6. Egg-shaped; come up
7. Turncoat
8. Slogan; lover's meeting
9. Compassion
10. Plot; shrewd
11. Foot digit; loan; chest bone
12. Canopy; dog's home
13. Mourning poem
14. Put off; noxious
15. Receive eagerly
16. Abrupt; express gratitude
17. Governor; fantasy
18. Train track; proportion; ___ of Dogs, London area
19. Complain; public
20. Put on record; steep in vinegar; negotiation
21. Go in; blunder

| S | C | H |
|---|---|---|
| T | O | E |
| A | W | N |

| ■ | T | R |
|---|---|---|
| T | O | ■ |
| E | ■ | H |

| E | ■ | M |
|---|---|---|
| T | N | A |
| E | ■ | N |

| I | T | A |
|---|---|---|
| L | ■ | C |
| L | ■ | I |

| ■ | R | ■ |
|---|---|---|
| D | E | T |
| ■ | ■ | E |

| C | O | F |
|---|---|---|
| L | ■ | L |
| O | G | U |

| A | X | I |
|---|---|---|
| L | ■ | L |
| O | V | A |

| I | ■ | B |
|---|---|---|
| F | I | L |
| F | ■ | E |

| V | E | R |
|---|---|---|
| E | ■ | D |
| R | R | O |

| E | ■ | N |
|---|---|---|
| R | ■ | D |
| A | T | I |

| ■ | ■ | N |
|---|---|---|
| M | O | T |
| U | ■ | ■ |

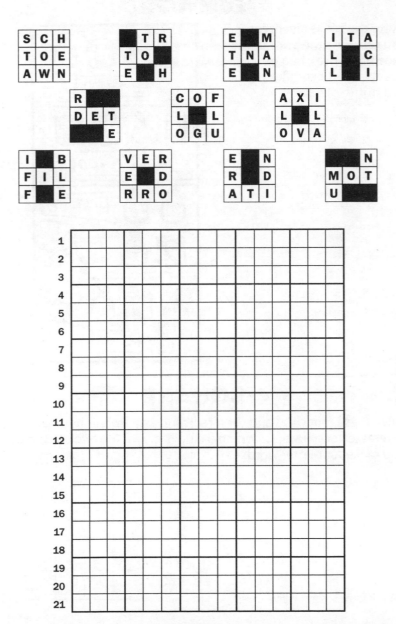

| 1 |
| 2 |
| 3 |
| 4 |
| 5 |
| 6 |
| 7 |
| 8 |
| 9 |
| 10 |
| 11 |
| 12 |
| 13 |
| 14 |
| 15 |
| 16 |
| 17 |
| 18 |
| 19 |
| 20 |
| 21 |

See answer 198

# SUM-UP

Using the totals given, can you calculate the price of each tin of peas, bag of sweets, box of cornflakes and bottle of milk?

£ 5 - 50

£ 6 - 00

£ 5 - 50

£ 6 - 00

8

# 4-SQUARE

Solve these four clues and then rearrange the solutions into a sixteen-letter phrase, for which a clue is given. The two diagonals also make four-letter words.

DIPLOMACY

FEMALE HORSE

SWORD HANDLE

BELONGING TO ME

Clue: Maths on the brain? (6,10)

*See answer 198-199*

# KEYWORD

This puzzle has no clues in the conventional sense. Instead, every different number printed in the main grid represents a different letter (with the same number always representing the same letter, of course). For example, if 7 turns out to be a 'V', you can write in V wherever a square contains 7. We have completed a very small part of the puzzle to give you a start, but the rest is up to you.

| 18 | 11 | 1 | 8 | 15 | 4 (T) | | 24 | 8 | 14 | 13 | 23 | 1 |
| 2 | | 21 | | 17 | 8 (A) | 22 | 2 | 3 | | 23 | | 9 |
| 25 | 8 | 10 | 4 | 23 | 14 (R) | | 4 | 21 | 1 | 26 | 23 | 4 |
| 2 | | 2 | | 7 | | | | 13 | | 17 | | 6 |
| 10 | 8 | 3 | 6 | 2 | 14 | | 4 | 17 | 21 | 2 | 12 | 2 |
| 4 | 14 | 11 | | 18 | 2 | 26 | 23 | 4 | | 14 | 8 | 13 |
| | 15 | | | | 12 | | 19 | | | | 3 | |
| 16 | 23 | 8 | | 1 | 2 | 5 | 9 | 15 | | 15 | 9 | 16 |
| 9 | 1 | 14 | 2 | 8 | 3 | | 2 | 8 | 15 | 21 | 2 | 14 |
| 3 | | 16 | | 4 | | | | 6 | | 13 | | 2 |
| 13 | 1 | 23 | 6 | 21 | 10 | | 15 | 26 | 23 | 1 | 13 | 2 |
| 2 | | 9 | | 12 | 23 | 7 | 2 | 3 | | 2 | | 22 |
| 18 | 8 | 14 | 20 | 2 | 1 | | 13 | 2 | 1 | 4 | 3 | 11 |

## A B C D E F G H I J K L M
## N O P Q R S T U V W X Y Z

(The small grid is provided for ease of reference only)

| 1 | 2 | 3 | 4 | 5 | 6 | 7 | 8 | 9 | 10 | 11 | 12 | 13 |
| 14 | 15 | 16 | 17 | 18 | 19 | 20 | 21 | 22 | 23 | 24 | 25 | 26 |

See answer 199

# CONTINUITY

No black squares – heavy bars mark the ends of words.

## ACROSS

1 Legendary creature also known as the Yeti (10,7)

2 Present; follow closely; slate; vein of metal

3 Infirmary; calf meat; crowded

4 Everlasting; educational talk; spinning toy

5 Preferably; Kentish kiln; football teams

6 Die; peculiar; small imperial weight; metal container

7 Churchman; reply; recount

8 Item of photographic equipment; upright; undisclosed fact

9 Affix; prophet; lubricate; apportion

10 Javelin; irritate; balms

11 Individual; East Midlands county town; prickling sensation

12 Immeasurable; thick mist; cereal plant

13 Say more; garden barrier; rebelling; upper limb

14 Pleasantly; gossip; punitive

15 Scrutinise; make into law; too; Ireland

16 Weird; ___heel, weak spot; firearm

17 Showy flower; quick look; nocturnal flying mammal; vital body organ

## DOWN

1 Stuck to; largest inland salt lake (7,3)

2 Car's trunk; chopper; footnotes

3 Beginning; cosseted; farm vehicle

4 Chart; Cologne's river; young girl; Aladdin's spirit friend

5 Journey plan; duty list; lascivious look

6 Mesh; stadium; soundness of mind; short sleep

7 Having nothing to do (2,1,5,3); threaten

8 Love-song; bird on a farthing; aural pain

9 Exists; antlered animal; planet's path; gratuity

10 Voter; modestly shy; ink smudge; white vestment

11 Condition; up to which time; however; ___ Fitzgerald, singer

12 Nothing; forearm bone; postbox aperture; conifer; solidify

13 Aged; leisure activity; Victoria Beckham's Spice name

14 Tiny; always; ___ film, food wrap; farm birds

15 Monaco's capital (5,5); crushed ice dessert

16 Illegal fire-raising; consumed; merely; less common

17 ___ and tatties, Scottish vegetable dish; after deductions; appear; period before Easter

*See answer 199*

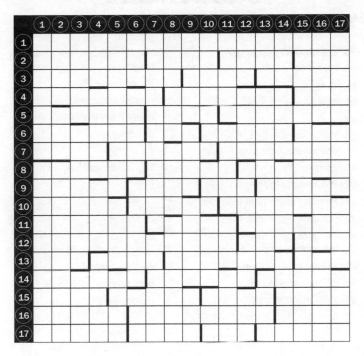

# RIDDLE-ME-REE

My first is in BATH but not in LOCK-UP,

My second's in HOT CHOCOLATE never in CUP,

My third's in both DOZY and DUVET,

My fourth's in HIT THE though not in HAY,

My fifth's in UNWIND and also PILLOW,

My sixth is in DREAMS but not RADIO,

My seventh's in EXTINGUISH but not seen in LIGHTS,

My whole is the hour that we retire at nights.

See answer 199

# CROSSWORD

**ACROSS**

1 Ox-like (6)

5 Unpleasantly sticky (6)

9 Since (3)

11 Corrupter (7)

12 Collide with (3,4)

13 Well ventilated (4)

15 Large piece of cotton used as bed clothing (5)

16 Saunter (4)

17 Wrestling hold (4)

19 Painting implement (5)

20 Off-white gemstone (4)

24 Thing which is said to be the lowest form of wit (7)

25 Experienced person (3,4)

26 ___ up, confess (3)

27 Detection device (6)

28 Number in a football team (6)

**DOWN**

2 Edict (5)

3 Small measurement of length (4)

4 Minor quake (5,6)

5 Pivotal person or thing (11)

6 Female relative (4)

7 Craziness (5)

8 Found (9)

10 Stone deposited by an avalanche (9)

14 Tibetan ox (3)

16 Romance (3)

18 Slice (5)

21 Tableware item (5)

22 Pierces, stabs (4)

23 Blade's sharpened side (4)

See answer 199

# TINKER, TAILOR ...

To discover who this person is unscramble the words in the verse, which hints at what the person does. Write these words into the boxes below, reading across, and, if you've placed them in the correct order, the arrowed column will spell out the occupation.

This CANDER can PALE and POTURIEET,

So gracefully whether LOOS or in a duet.

SQUAREBEA, CHATTEREN whatever POISONIT she is in,

Her MORNPERFACE leaves her UNICADEE in a spin.

OCCUPATION: _____ _____

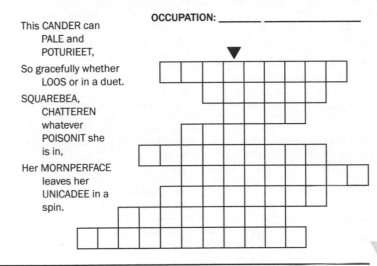

# SILHOUETTE

Shade in every fragment containing a dot – and what have you got?

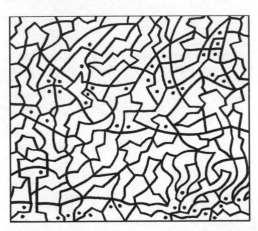

*See answer 199*

# STORY CROSSWORD

Transfer the words which complete the story to the grid and then put the circled letters in the right order to discover the name of the famous person therein described.

He was ___ (16A) in Grand Chute, Wisconsin, in 1908 and was ___ (13D) at Marquette University. He worked as a lawyer after graduating, then became a circuit-court judge in 1939. When America was drawn into World War II, he joined the US ___ (7A) Corps and served in the Pacific. He reached the ___ (9A) of captain.

In 1946 he was elected to the US Senate as a member of the Republican party. This was an era in which rumours were beginning to circulate about the way ___ (1A) infiltrators were becoming ___ (21A) in public life. An investigation was launched into these allegations and a number of high-profile trials were held.

Four years later, in 1950, he decided to ___ (4D) out about his ___ (5D) that there were communists working in the Department of State. The allegations ___ (8A) him a great deal of public attention and he continued to accuse high-ranking figures of communist sympathies, though his claims were never substantiated.

In 1953 he was appointed chairman of a Senate ___ (1D) which was given the task of conducting investigations into un-American activities. His determination to root out communists at ___ (21D) cost ___ (23A) many of his colleagues and ___ (3D) the public. He conducted extremely thorough enquiries into the activities of ___ (18A) of his suspects and made ___ (2D) and more accusations. He even ___ (11D) the possibility that President Eisenhower might be involved.

In 1954 he accused the Secretary of the Army of concealing foreign espionage activities. The allegation brought about a backlash that he had not ___ (14D). The Secretary claimed that members of his committee ___ (6D) threatened army officials with investigation if they would not give preferential treatment to a committee consultant who had ___ (20D) been drafted.

He denied ___ (12A) charge, but an inquiry into his own activities was ___ (17A) up. It did not ___ (10A) likely that his political career could survive such a blow, especially as the press gave the matter wide publicity. He would not allow himself to ___ (19D) on the likely outcome of the case, but kept insisting on his innocence. In the end he was cleared of the charges, but the Senate ruled that he had ___ (19A) considerable harm to a number of senators in his investigations. He was allowed to ___ (22A) to the Senate, but his influence was considerably reduced.

He ___ (15A) in office in 1957.

See answer 199

# BOXWISE

Put these three-letter groups into the twelve numbered boxes to produce twelve six-letter words, each of which starts in one box and finishes in another as indicated by an arrow. For instance, 2 and 5 make a six-letter word, but not 5 and 9. One group has been filled in to start you off.

BAL ~~CHO~~ DER GEN

KEN LAD PON SEN

SIL TRY VER WEA

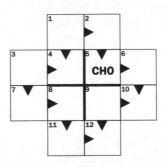

*See answer 199*

21

# WORDSEARCH

The 45 words from the works of William Shakespeare have all been hidden in the diagram. They have been printed across (backwards or forwards), or up or down, or diagonally, but always in a straight line without letters being skipped. You can use the letters in the diagram more than once. You will probably find it helpful to mark the words in the diagram and cross them off the list as you find them.

```
O N W L V N E D A E R H T G T F
P O L L U S I O N W O B R N X E
R T U E G F P S A X I E E D S I
E H I E R A E L W B E D E I T H
R I G R S U L T B I A I G S A T
A N E H R E T L A C N N L E N R
U G S U Y I E F I B I D C D D E
Q G T E G B T L A M A N G G E T
S I D C A N D L E W A S T E R A
M F C B T T O E P T F U H N B W
U T B O J N S T R A R R F E Y M
R L A Z T E H O P E N P U R N G
E Z L R U L P C I S L D R S E T
E D E R X A W S E E A B E I H Y
J U T T Y K O E N E K W M R M F
D E Z A R C E R A C K I D U L Y
E Z I O P A R I T O R P L B R Y
F A D G E J E U R G N O C G H D
```

| | | | |
|---|---|---|---|
| BALE | FADGE | NOTHING-GIFT | TANE |
| BATEFUL | FRUSH | PANDERLY | THREADEN |
| BIBBLE-BABBLE | GALLIMAUFREY | PARITOR | TIRRIT |
| CADENT | GEST | PASH | TOAZE |
| CANDLE-WASTER | GLIKE | POIZE | TRUE-SEEMING |
| CARE-CRAZED | GREE | POLLUSION | WAFTURE |
| CONGRUE | HOX | PORTANCE | WALL-EYED |
| COSIER | JACK-A-LENT | PRIMY | WASP-TONGUE |
| DISEDGE | JUTTY | SHENT | WATER-THIEF |
| DRUMBLE | KEECH | SQUARER | WAX-RED |
| ESCOT | LEESE | STANDER-BY | |
| | MURE | SWINDGE | |

*See answer 200*

# NUMBER JIG

Just like a Jig-word – but instead of letters, numbers.

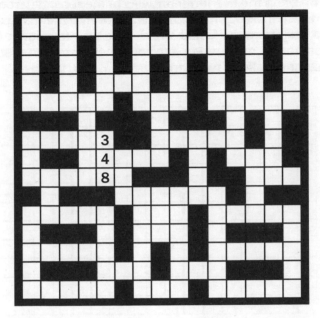

| **3-figure** | **4-figure** | 23099 | 70913 |
|---|---|---|---|
| 114 | 1039 | 23136 | 83146 |
| 163 | 2430 | 23368 | 87111 |
| 246 | 3926 | 25007 | 91060 |
| 348 | 6911 | 34261 | 96203 |
| 407 | | 39130 | |
| 410 | | 43162 | |
| 508 | **5-figure** | 43915 | **6-figure** |
| 511 | 10150 | 52289 | 216345 |
| 607 | 10992 | 52617 | 347288 |
| 625 | 12074 | 61134 | 513084 |
| 745 | 13412 | 61408 | 624397 |
| 834 | 15918 | 65052 | 711642 |
| 863 | 17102 | 65054 | |
| 914 | 19066 | 70234 | |

*See answer 200*

# BRACER

The first part of each clue gives a six-letter answer, five of whose letters make up the five-letter answers to the second part and four of which make up the four-letter answer to the third part. The unused letter from the first answer is entered into column A, and that from the second answer into column B. When completed, the two columns spell out two games.

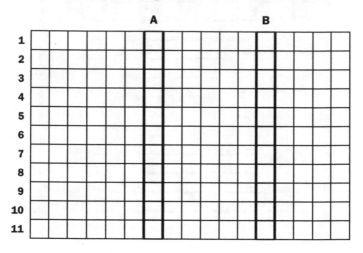

1 Gnawing mammal; male bee; swelling or bulge

2 Spoil, harm; ___donna, singer; prudish

3 Cot; apparent; authentic

4 Pace; take exam again; remainder

5 Pilfered; pebble; foot digits

6 Spin; hearth; rip

7 Totter, shuffle; muddle; go in front

8 Tooth decay; concerns; motor vehicles

9 Cloak; alloy; deceased

10 Close-fitting necklace; task; Sonny's former singing partner

11 ___ up, nervously tense; pig's noise; garden basket

*See answer 200*

# SPIRAL

Every answer (except the first) uses the last letter of the preceding answer as its initial letter, the chain thus formed following a spiral path to the centre of the grid. The diagonals spell two materials.

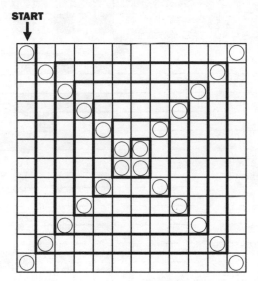

- Well-mannered (9)
- Ill-health (8)
- Indian Ocean islands (10)
- Natural sweetener (5)
- Out of work, surplus (9)
- Canadian city (7)
- Fruit and colour (6)
- Physical training (8)
- European country (7)
- Samson's treacherous mistress (7)
- After-school study (8)
- Fate (6)
- Inn (6)

- Pest, irritation (8)
- Excitable, fiery (9)
- Tree with poisonous pods (8)
- Supervisor (7)
- WW2 desert leader of German army (6)
- CS ___, author of the *Narnia* books (5)
- Rebuff, slight (4)
- Infuse tea (4)
- Royal Prince (7)
- Flying insect (4)
- Lobby (4)
- Cooking fat (4)
- Colouring (3)

*See answer 200*

# CROSSWORD

## ACROSS

**1** Cajun dish (5)

**4** Food tin (3)

**6** Pale, tired (6,3)

**7** Prosperous (4-2-2)

**9** Tequila cocktail (9)

**10** Stole (4)

**12** Succour (4)

**14** Confuse, mystify (8)

**17** Lazy (8)

**19** Pitch black (4)

**21** Stick together (4)

**23** Middle of a large centre of population (5,4)

**25** Fire-raiser (8)

**27** List of all stock (9)

**28** No goals (3)

**29** From what source? (5)

## DOWN

**1** Academic vestment (4)

**2** Therapist (7)

**3** On the other side of the page (8)

**4** Double file of pupils (9)

**5** Protected area of countryside (8,4)

**8** Soot particles (5)

**11** Style of music associated with Pavarotti (5)

**13** Scottish fjord (5)

**15** Malignant spirit (5)

**16** Complex human society (12)

**18** Blue-green gemstone (5)

**20** Old name for scrofula (5,4)

**22** Up to the minute (5,3)

**24** Available at the supermarket (2-5)

**26** Computing term for memory size (4)

*See answer 200*

# JIG-WORD

No clues – just pattern and answers – but can you fit them in?

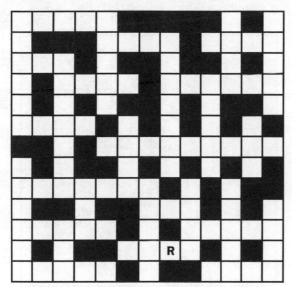

**3-letter words**
AGO
ASH
GEL
RUG
THE

**4-letter words**
DARE
HERE
ISLE
METE
OGLE
OOZE

SEER
SENT
TAIL
VOTE

**5-letter words**
ASKEW
CRUDE
EAGER
EVADE
FIEND
RAGED
TALON
THAWS
WORLD

**6-letter words**
ARREST
ASPECT
LIFTED

**7-letter words**
ENLARGE
GORILLA
SHATTER

**9-letter word**
LARGENESS

See answer 200

27

# DROP-OUT

In the top picture the girl is selecting an apron. In the bottom, she has made her purchase. Which apron did she buy?

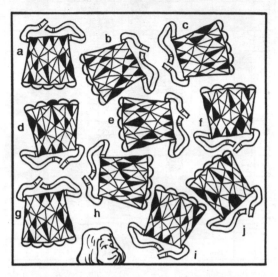

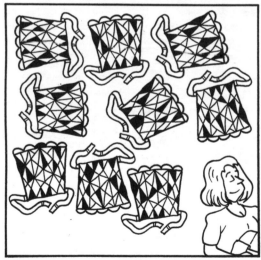

# CRYPTIC CROSSWORD

## ACROSS

1 Striking worker? (10)
6 Sour drop that's sweet (4)
9 Remove a surface with difficulty immediately (3,4)
10 Where do fashionable patients go? (7)
12 Exploit opportunity to gain point on court (4,9)
14 How about a right-left combination in Essex? (6)
15 Like finest, outstanding, incombustible material (8)
17 Holy fish? (8)
19 Roughly score about 100, but not in this game? (6)
22 S-sea (8,5)
24 Twelfth man's shyness (7)
25 Bird spotted account (7)
26 Fighting military initially who are ardent (4)
27 Advance settlement (10)

## DOWN

1 Exclude new outbuilding (4)
2 Judge had rarebit ordered (7)
3 Construct hastily despite strike at the same time (5,8)
4 Done with the hands by the book? (6)
5 Tending to take from this hive? (8)
7 Scoundrel to rave over fruit (7)
8 I send spray from chemist's shop (10)
11 Fly-past? (6,4,3)
13 Tom's company in a painful squeeze (10)
16 Listen again to words of approval (4,4)
18 Naval boxing weight? (7)
20 Imprison criminal with penalty (7)
21 Talk of pigs so violent (6)
23 Bachelor had many a black mark (4)

See answer 201

# TWO-TIMER

Two sets of clues to the same answers. Cryptic clues below and straight clues beneath the grid.

## ACROSS

**1** Finest journey on horseback? (8)

**5** Tax man? (4)

**9** Light twinkler? (7)

**10** Harshly criticise the Spanish team (5)

**11** Amphibian found in leftovers (3)

**12** Rubbish bride removed before Saturday (6)

**15** Said I otherwise had included dolt (5)

**17** Solo performance in the city (4)

**19** Blush in colourful study (6)

**22** In the way a learner set up office (6)

**24** Something boring to do when sleepy? (4)

**26** Ride round (5)

**27** Comment about smear (6)

**30** Clearing some of the meadow (3)

**32** A doctor in the British Isles initially had a deer (5)

**33** Story about equality Abel misconstrued (7)

**34** Tax ring (4)

**35** Broken platters make a mess! (8)

## DOWN

**1** Only one per person but several people can make it (4)

**2** Pen the French type (5)

**3** Revolutionary palindrome (5)

**4** Rude development on ship leads to imprisonment (6)

**6** Include studies first (7)

**7** Sign of person revealing info? (4-4)

**8** On top I arranged selection (6)

**13** Shoot pal (3)

**14** First person said to be proprietor of island (4)

**16** Criticism about missile (8)

**18** Trade route (4)

**20** Point mistakenly claimed (7)

**21** Its closure prevents one seeing (6)

**23** Spain out? Try Bath (3)

**25** Be quiet – put on a cover presently! (4,2)

**28** Among the calamari, a girl appeared (5)

**29** Disprove engineer's objection (5)

**31** One who lives for drink? (4)

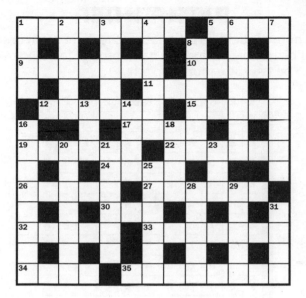

## ACROSS

1 Sit across (8)
5 Caledonian (4)
9 Poetic word for the sun (7)
10 Jury (5)
11 Newt (3)
12 Wreckage (6)
15 Fool (5)
17 Norwegian capital (4)
19 Flush (6)
22 Place in an official seat (6)
24 Gape (4)
26 Bike (5)
27 Observation (6)
30 Pasture (3)
32 Film about a baby deer (5)
33 Biblical moral tale (7)
34 Road levy (4)
35 Smear with blobs (8)

## DOWN

1 Torso (4)
2 Fashion (5)
3 Helicopter's blade (5)
4 Constraint (6)
6 Comprise (7)
7 Sneak (4-4)
8 Choice (6)
13 Partly opened flower (3)
14 Hebridean isle (4)
16 Uncomplimentary remark (8)
18 Bar (4)
20 In tens (7)
21 Optical cover (6)
23 Health resort (3)
25 Settle completely (4,2)
28 Black ___, prison van (5)
29 Refute (5)
31 Ale (4)

*See answer 201*

# PATHFINDER

Starting from the bold centre letter, move up or down or sideways (but NOT diagonally) to find the path through fourteen things or people to be seen on a football pitch.

| E | E | R | E | R | C | L | E | L | P | O |
|---|---|---|---|---|---|---|---|---|---|---|
| R | C | T | C | I | E | W | S | A | O | S |
| E | E | N | R | E | E | A | L | L | G | T |
| F | U | O | T | P | P | B | U | T | I | S |
| E | C | K | E | E | E | R | T | E | T | U |
| R | H | L | A | O | **G** | N | E | P | S | B |
| R | L | I | N | T | L | A | F | R | E | N |
| A | S | O | E | Y | E | M | L | A | G | R |
| B | S | R | C | S | N | I | D | F | C | O |
| T | S | T | O | P | I | L | L | I | R | E |
| R | I | K | E | R | G | O | A | E | L | D |

# DOT-TO-DOT

Join the dots in numerical order to reveal the hidden picture.

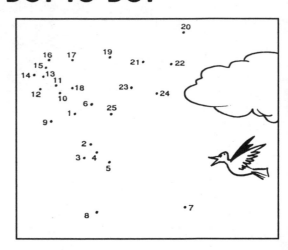

See answer 201

# CROSSWORD

**ACROSS**

1 Dry run (8)

6 Control in an unfair way (9)

7 Of advanced years (3)

8 Cantankerous (5)

9 Alp (8)

12 Kiln for drying hops (4)

13 Mark for life (4)

16 Coastal swamp (4,5)

18 Person watching a game (9)

19 Taverns (4)

20 Pinnacle (4)

23 Drug which causes sleep or relieves pain (8)

26 Hard, leavened, ring-shaped roll (5)

27 Part of a bridle (3)

28 Make entire (9)

29 Time of need (5,3)

**DOWN**

1 Decorative woollen tassel (6)

2 Unremitting (9)

3 Cantering (8)

4 ___ bun, sticky cake (7)

5 Uniquely (4)

10 Someone living closer to the Arctic (10)

11 Crime of having an illegal drug about one's person (10)

14 Unit of fineness of gold (5)

15 Concord (5)

17 Sleep late (3,2)

21 Reconstructed wood made from cuttings (9)

22 Vandal (8)

24 Boating event (7)

25 Unflinching (6)

26 Money paid to the courts as security (4)

*See answer 201*

# BACKWARDS

For this puzzle, we've filled in the answers, but there are letters in the grid, where the black squares should be. You need to black out the unwanted letters to make a symmetrical grid to match the clues, which are listed in random order.

| S | O | B | U | S | I | N | A | P | I | G |
|---|---|---|---|---|---|---|---|---|---|---|
| E | R | I | M | P | R | O | V | E | M | U |
| E | B | B | R | A | I | D | E | W | A | N |
| D | R | E | A | T | D | O | N | E | B | B |
| P | A | L | Y | L | E | A | D | A | S | P |
| A | D | O | L | E | S | C | E | N | C | E |
| N | A | G | A | I | C | E | N | D | O | T |
| T | W | O | L | D | E | L | E | I | N | E |
| O | L | D | E | A | N | T | W | A | D | D |
| R | E | R | A | U | C | O | U | S | P | A |
| B | A | Y | A | K | E | Y | A | K | I | D |

**ACROSS**

— Small insect
— Friend
— Get better
— Young goat
— Drink cooler
— Pale
— Weep, cry
— Teenage years
— Ancient
— Poisonous snake
— Give assistance
— Farm animal
— Combine numbers
— Meadow
— Harsh, hoarse
— Harass
— Commit an act of wickedness
— Unlocking device
— Small spot
— Flow back
— Leaf used in cooking

**DOWN**

— Bulky piece of wood
— Sign of agreement
— Parent
— Baby's clothes protector
— Multi-coloured shimmer
— Also
— Firearm
— Greek god of pastures
— Health resort
— Flee, hide
— Lacking moisture
— Catch sight of
— Plaything
— Boring tool
— Church seat
— Short-winged bird
— Domesticated animal
— Hawaiian garland
— Sphere
— Enquire
— High card

*See answer 201*

# JOLLY MIXTURES

In this puzzle, each clue is simply an anagram of the answer – but watch out! There might be more than one possible solution to each clue. For instance, the clue 'TALE' might lead to the answer 'LATE' or 'TEAL'. You'll have to look at how the answers fit into the grid to find out which alternative is correct.

**ACROSS**

| | |
|---|---|
| 1 LEAP | 21 MEAD |
| 5 CHAR | 22 POLEMIC |
| 8 ALOFT | 23 SHAM |
| 10 HOOTS | 25 TERN |
| 11 LONER | 28 RON |
| 12 ORB | 30 LIVED |
| 14 MARE | 32 RINGO |
| 17 BALE | 33 SONAR |
| 19 LEADING | 34 PROD |
| 20 ARTS | 35 SUED |

**DOWN**

| | |
|---|---|
| 2 ALOOF | 16 CHARM |
| 3 FAT | 17 DREAD |
| 4 LOOP | 18 MELON |
| 5 TEA | 23 DOME |
| 6 COBRA | 24 VERSE |
| 7 RATS | 26 DOREE |
| 9 FUEL | 27 GNAT |
| 12 LAMINAR | 29 STOA |
| 13 INBREED | 31 ALP |
| 15 RETAX | 32 GUN |

*See answer 201*

# DOUBLE CROSS

When the letters of the answers from the upper grid are transferred to the lower grid, they give a quotation. Reading down column 'A' will give the name of its author.

|   |   | A | B | C | D | E | F | G | H | J | K |
|---|---|---|---|---|---|---|---|---|---|---|---|
| 1 | Cellar | | | | | | | | | | |
| 2 | In front; worry | | | | | | | | | | |
| 3 | Wages; pigpen | | | | | | | | | | |
| 4 | Deduce; widespread | | | | | | | | | | |
| 5 | Torpid | | | | | | | | | | |
| 6 | Hunting dog; impolite | | | | | | | | | | |
| 7 | Result; offer | | | | | | | | | | |
| 8 | Trivial; employment | | | | | | | | | | |
| 9 | Contemplate | | | | | | | | | | |

| 5D | 7A | 8A | 3B | 4B |    | 5A | 7E | 9C | 4K |    | 5H | 3A |    |    |
|----|----|----|----|----|----|----|----|----|----|----|----|----|----|----|
| 4E | 9H | 8G | 1B | 3E | 2E | 7J | 6D | 5G |    | 4C | 6B | 8E |    | 4H | 3J |
| 7H | 6G | 8B | 9G | 2B | 5C | 4D | 1G | 3H |    | 6H | 7B |    | 7F | 6A | 1D |
| 6J | 2A | 3F |    | 3D | 9B | 6E |    | 1E | 5E | 8K | 9A | 7C |    |    |    |
| 2K | 7D | 1F |    | 1A | 6C | 2H | 7K | 5B | 8C | 9E |    |    |    |    |    |
| 8H | 2G |    | 3C | 9D | 4J | 2C |    | 6K | 9F | 1C | 4A | 2J | 5F |    |    |
| 1H | 8D |    | 5J | 2D | 4G | 8J | 3K |    |    |    |    |    |    |    |    |
|    |    |    |    |    |    | .  |    |    |    |    |    |    |    |    |    |

See answer 202

# TINKER, TAILOR ...

To discover who this person is unscramble the words in the verse, which hints at what the person does. Write these words into the boxes below, reading across, and, if you've placed them in the correct order, the arrowed column will spell out the occupation.

He's the RGDNAE PREXTE you will need to call

When your KOA, MEL or CEHBE WRGOS a little too LALT.

He'll TUC the HSRNCBEA with a powerful INACHAWS,

So your outdoor retreat is TANE and tidy once more.

OCCUPATION: _____

# 4-SQUARE

Solve these four clues and then rearrange the solutions into a sixteen-letter phrase, for which a clue is given. The two diagonals also make four-letter words.

ROMAN CATHOLIC CHURCH SERVICE

CLOAK

CUTLERY ITEM

WEED

Clue: An indication of admiration (2,1,4,2,7)

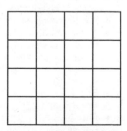

*See answer 202*

# ROUND TOUR

A fantastic puzzle in which each square counts at least twice – some count three or four times! The answer-words form two continuous chains, each of them starting at the top left-hand corner and following the directions of the arrows to and fro along alternate rows, and down and up along alternate columns. Moreover, the last letter of one word is the first letter of the next one. For example, the three consecutive words GINGER, RED and DAVID would appear in the completed puzzle as GINGEREDAVID, so be careful – it's not an easy puzzle!

## TO AND FRO

- Urgent ironing (8)
- Queen glows about scowls (7)
- Divides stocks (6)
- Captain's jumper? (7)
- Enlarge bore of 500 sheets (4)
- Tim nets new gloves (7)
- Starts care onboard (6)
- Mark musical composition (5)
- Mire muddied Arabian ruler (4)
- Relax area of responsibility (5)
- Lawrence has a leaf infusion (3)
- Horrify a quiet pal (5)
- Thin incline (4)
- Salamander is new team leader (4)
- Rests twisted lock of hair (5)
- Second beer transaction (4)
- Previously disturbed rest (4)
- Dragged along to marry (5)
- Russian country house in Vologda chalet park (5)
- A gale entangled seaweeds (5)
- Finish last point (3)
- Far down river softly (4)
- Father in agony (4)
- More agreeable northern ice queen (5)
- Split hire charge (4)
- Follow scut (4)
- Miss Stansfield is in Los Angeles (4)

- Concerning a fight (5)
- Reportedly goes round seabirds (5)
- Slumbered or pole vaulted, we hear (5)
- Chinese groups attempt adverts, it's reported (6)
- Love as returned Portuguese saint (3)
- Circle ancient city belonging to us (3)
- Rummage for part of plant (4)
- Plaything to youth leader (3)
- Affirmative you old son! (3)
- Dry tasting moment (3)
- Visitor to telephone Her Majesty (6)
- Italian capital has old ladies' man (5)

## DOWN AND UP

- Allow me trip rearrangement (6)
- Hill to right (3)
- Peruse about advert (4)
- Performs new odes (4)
- Sews in repaired tendons (6)
- Expensive marinade (5)
- Get ready re paper reshuffle (7)
- Upright Crete construction (5)
- Time right morning transport (4)
- Debatable doctor has nil time (4)
- Thanks one from Bangkok (3)
- Aide altered concept (4)

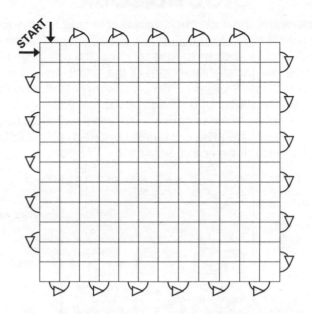

- Point at objective (3)
- Fail to meet girl (4)
- Economise on politician après ski (5)
- Organise blueprint (4)
- Bite Ulster political leader (3)
- Purr about eastern cleaner (5)
- Eric left weird antiquity (5)
- About soft peaked hat (3)
- Step around tame animals (4)
- Pole in evil act (3)
- Mesh after tax (3)
- Team leader spots rubbish (5)
- Greet icy shower (4)
- Look, fifty left lounge (4)
- See Saints defeat (4)
- Pass new baths (4)
- Sounds like unhurried blackthorn fruit (4)
- Hesitation before good work unit (3)
- Look briefly at ricochet (6)

- The Spanish go after eastern slippery customer (3)
- The French ant inclined (5)
- Coat cooked Mexican pancake ... (4)
- ... or bowled ball (3)
- Plead for British capital, for example (3)
- Inform about turf (5)
- Displays how onboard ship (5)
- Dispatched, it's said, for perfume (5)
- Thanks Danish leader a little bit (3)
- Female deer do point (3)
- Observes votes in favour, we hear (4)
- Solidify group (3)
- Sounds like 20cwt cask (3)
- Inside mine were more up-to-date (5)
- Seldom found undercooked (4)

See answer 202

# TRIO

Can you spot the three identical vases?

# 36

# TAKE FIVE

The three answers in this mini-crossword read the same across and down. We've given you clues to the three words, but NOT in the right order. See how quickly you can solve it.

**1** Constellation containing seven bright stars

**2** Stretched tight, strained

**3** Freshwater fish of the salmon genus

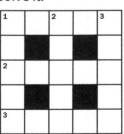

*See answer 202*

# KEYWORD

This puzzle has no clues in the conventional sense. Instead, every different number printed in the main grid represents a different letter (with the same number always representing the same letter, of course). For example, if 7 turns out to be a 'V', you can write in V wherever a square contains 7. We have completed a very small part of the puzzle to give you a start, but the rest is up to you.

| 23 | 24 | 9 | 1 | 4 | | | 24 | | 7 | 10 | 19 | 21 | 24 |
|----|----|----|----|----|----|----|----|----|----|----|----|----|----|
| 6 | | 10 | | 13 | 3 | 2 | 3 | 24 | | 2 | | | 17 |
| 1 | 10 | 6 | 24 | 10 | | 1 | | 1 | 25 | 3 | 26 | 24 |
| 17 | | 4 | | 24 | 22 | 19 | 13 | 24 | | 23 | | | 18 |
| | 4 | 16 | 6 | 24 | 5 | 22 | | 4 | 14 | 24 | 22 | 22 |
| 15 | | 6 | | | 1 | | 24 | | 19 | | | 5 |
| 5 | 12 | 24 | 20 | 6 | 24 | | 11 | 24 | 25 | 24 | 22 | 4 |
| 10 | | | 24 | | 2 | | 24 | | | 2 | | 4 |
| 9 | 24 | 4 | 24 | 1 | | 4 | 26 | 5 | 20 | 1 | 17 | |
| 22 | | 14 | | 14 | 24 | 5 | 1 | 4 | | 10 | | 19 |
| 3 | 15 | 5 | 18 | 19 | | 12 | | 13 P | 22 | 6 | 26 | 8 |
| 20 | | 8 | | 10 | 24 | 24 | 12 | 24 E | | 23 | | 5 |
| 18 | 22 | 24 | 5 | 20 | | 10 | | 20 N | 24 | 24 | 23 | 17 |

A B C D E F G H I J K L M
N O P Q R S T U V W X Y Z

(The small grid is provided for ease of reference only)

| 1 | 2 | 3 | 4 | 5 | 6 | 7 | 8 | 9 | 10 | 11 | 12 | 13 |
|----|----|----|----|----|----|----|----|----|----|----|----|----|
| 14 | 15 | 16 | 17 | 18 | 19 | 20 | 21 | 22 | 23 | 24 | 25 | 26 |

*See answer 202*

# CROSSWORD

## ACROSS

1 Aits (5)
4 Supremely regal (8)
11 Imbue, instil (9)
12 Garden shelter (5)
13 Dusted with sugar (4)
14 Cowled (6)
16 Piste runner (3)
18 Give money to (3)
19 Pie, tart etc (6)
22 Crumbly earthy mixture used as a fertiliser (4)
24 Japanese art of swordsmanship (5)
26 Winter garment (9)
27 Art of witty replies (8)
28 Quick, nimble (5)

## DOWN

2 Impressive (7)
3 Towards the rising of the sun (4)
5 Alter for the good (5)
6 Incorporate (6)
7 Raw fibres of hemp and flax (3)
8 Personal warmth (10)
9 Card game where the loser undresses (5,5)
10 Board-game with counters (4)
15 ___ for, select (3)
16 Block up (4,3)
17 Commotion (6)
20 Uninterrupted transition from one piece of music or film to another (5)
21 Sea hazard often made of coral (4)
23 Pack (4)
25 Pinch, squeeze sharply (3)

*See answer 202*

# MISSING LINKS

The answer to each clue is a word which has a link with each of the three words listed. This word may come at the end (eg Head linked with Beach, Big and Hammer), at the beginning (eg Black linked with Beauty, Board and Jack) or a mixture of the two (eg Stone linked with Hail, Lime and Wall).

**ACROSS**
1 Band, Brighton, Cake (4)
3 Boy, Cruiser, Log (5)
6 Bottoms, Rope, Tent (4)
8 Falls, Plum, Queen (8)
10 Court, Elbow, Table (6)
11 Corn, Snow, Soap (6)
12 Grass, Highway, Powers (5)
13 Finish, Stitch, Wood (5)
15 Coffee, Dislike, Success (7)
18 Farm, Poker, Press (4)
19 Drop, Rain, Test (4)
20 Nelson, Rear, Red (7)
23 Birthday, Garden, Labour (5)
25 Box, Break, Liquid (5)
26 Murder, Sheepdog, Time (6)
28 Begging, Box, Love (6)
29 Compound, Rate, Vested (8)
31 Ice, Stock, Sugar (4)
32 Dresser, Rarebit, Terrier (5)
33 Chicken, High, Netting (4)

**DOWN**
1 Arms, Gear, Order (7)
2 Bag, Football, Tool (3)
3 Christmas, Service, Singing (5)
4 Bath, Electric, Wet (7)
5 Bank, Compare, Medical (5)
6 Republic, Skin, Split (6)
7 Driving, Object, Piano (6)
9 Chip, Personal, Programme (8)
11 Girl, Good, Man (6)
13 Choir, Market, Orchestra (6)
14 Bermuda, Equilateral, Eternal (8)
16 Lump, Round, Total (3)
17 Force, Mail, Pocket (3)
21 Letter, Reaction, Response (7)
22 Blower, Penny, Wolf (7)
23 Eye, Library, Servant (6)
24 Dove, Mock, Turn (6)
26 Away, Back, Over (5)
27 Key, Night, On (5)
30 Deal, Materials, Recruits (3)

 43

*See answer 202*

# BLACK OUT

Can you see which two artefacts are shown in silhouette at the top?

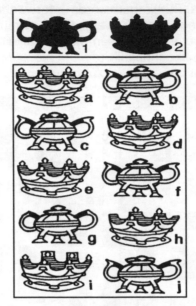

# SILHOUETTE

Shade in every fragment containing a dot – and what have you got?

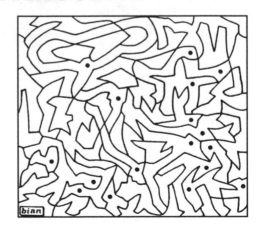

*See answer 202-203*

# WORDSEARCH

The 40 legal terms have all been hidden in the diagram. They have been printed across (backwards or forwards), or up or down, or diagonally, but always in a straight line without letters being skipped. You can use the letters in the diagram more than once. You will probably find it helpful to mark the words in the diagram and cross them off the list as you find them.

```
V  H  A  Y  S  Q  T  A  F  L  Y  A  B  U  Z  T
S  E  L  F  L  U  D  O  I  I  N  E  I  L  E  R
A  K  R  I  F  V  P  C  R  E  O  T  A  S  E  E
V  P  B  D  O  I  I  R  O  T  M  T  T  G  N  B
H  E  P  C  I  D  D  P  O  Y  I  A  R  R  J  M
L  T  A  E  O  C  B  A  R  C  T  U  X  U  G  A
D  T  A  C  A  U  T  A  V  E  S  O  C  A  O  H
E  C  W  O  S  L  I  P  M  I  E  A  V  R  C  C
T  N  E  M  T  C  I  D  N  I  T  E  E  N  I  W
W  Y  T  L  I  U  G  E  H  Y  L  Q  E  B  R  C
I  R  F  D  E  E  B  F  U  Z  S  B  L  I  A  I
T  U  U  K  C  D  B  A  R  R  I  S  T  E  R  H
N  J  T  A  N  I  W  M  E  T  U  T  A  T  S  F
E  P  E  V  E  C  C  A  L  U  M  N  Y  I  C  E
S  G  R  L  D  T  N  T  L  R  J  X  D  B  A  A
S  O  U  I  I  T  R  I  B  U  N  A  L  I  S  L
C  R  W  P  V  M  H  O  L  L  I  W  Y  L  E  T
S  I  L  K  E  Y  Q  N  F  B  T  R  I  A  L  Y
```

| | | | |
|---|---|---|---|
| ADVOCATE | CODICIL | JUDICIARY | SUBPOENA |
| AFFIDAVIT | COURT | JURY | TESTATE |
| ALIBI | DEFAMATION | LAW | TESTIMONY |
| APPEAL | EDICT | LIBEL | TORT |
| BARRISTER | EVIDENCE | LIEN | TRIAL |
| BENCH | FEALTY | OATH | TRIBUNAL |
| CALUMNY | GAVEL | PRIVY | VERDICT |
| CASE | GUILT | RULE | WILL |
| CHAMBER | HABEAS CORPUS | SILK | WITNESS |
| CIRCUIT | INDICTMENT | STATUTE | WRIT |

See answer 203

# NUMBER JIG

Just like a Jig-word – but instead of letters, numbers.

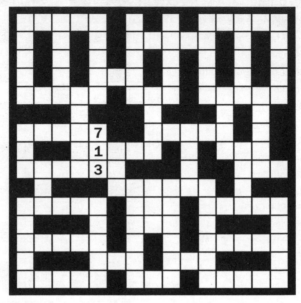

| 3-figure | 4-figure | 29161 | 86612 |
|----------|----------|-------|-------|
| 264 | 1284 | 30199 | 90839 |
| 286 | 2359 | 38008 | 92202 |
| 305 | 4850 | 43736 | 93126 |
| 362 | 8365 | 44233 | |
| 399 | | 48132 | |
| 468 | **5-figure** | 50104 | **6-figure** |
| 510 | 17904 | 51009 | 163982 |
| 516 | 18256 | 59216 | 293099 |
| 649 | 18891 | 60891 | 391136 |
| 713 | 20504 | 61200 | 425991 |
| 803 | 20609 | 63481 | 972141 |
| 917 | 21424 | 73033 | |
| 920 | 21837 | 80017 | |
| 981 | 28304 | 81011 | |

*See answer 203*

# CROSSWORD

## ACROSS

6 Docked (9)

7 Young snake-like fish (5)

8 Loud noise, racket (3)

9 Fashion (4)

10 Chinese religious statue (4)

12 Practice of being naked (8)

15 Half-yearly (8)

17 Throw away (7,2)

18 Lessen the severity of (8)

20 Brightness (of colours) (8)

23 Munch (4)

24 Piece of silicon in computers (4)

27 Be sickly (3)

28 Book containing recorded events of one year (5)

29 Animal money-box (5-4)

## DOWN

1 Running in a continuous current (9)

2 Arched (6)

3 Disdain (5)

4 Bookish (8)

5 Peculiarity (7)

11 Goods such as tools and household implements (11)

13 Matching sweater and cardigan (7)

14 Character on a musical stave (4)

16 Intact (7)

17 Female parents of animals (4)

19 Slim (5-4)

21 Way of thinking (8)

22 In bits and pieces (7)

25 Aerodrome shed (6)

26 Lecherous woodland being (5)

47

*See answer 203*

# STORY CROSSWORD

Transfer the words which complete the story to the grid and then put the circled letters in the right order to discover the name of the famous person therein described.

The ___ (5D) of a Lancashire cotton spinner who became a Labour MP, he was born in Stockport in 1909 and educated at Ealing County School in London. He ___ (17D) to play table tennis as a child, not realising that this would ___ (14D) him to international fame. His skill was so great, though, that by the ___ (10D) he was twenty, he was the world table-tennis champion.

He decided to take up tennis, a move which ___ (24A) many doors for him. He ___ (18A) hard at his ___ (22D) sport, modelling his techniques on those of the French player Henri Cochet. He was particularly ___ (22A) for the running forward ___ (3D) at which he excelled.

The ___ (13D) of his hard work was that he decided to ___ (19D) the Wimbledon tennis tournament in 1930. He beat the Italian ___ (11A) Umberto de Porpurgo in the third round. As a result of this performance, he was picked for the Davis ___ (15A) in Paris in 1933. He defeated Cochet and ___ (1D) won the trophy for the first time in twenty-one years.

In 1934 he beat the Australian Jack Crawford to win the Wimbledon singles title. His victory was to ___ (20A) members of the All-England Club and the Lawn Tennis

Association who ___ (12D) not come to terms with the idea of ___ (2D) from a working-class background becoming a champion. Despite the opposition of these ___ (12A), he ___ (6D) on with his game, winning Wimbledon in both 1935 and 1936.

He won the United States title in 1933, 1934 and 1936, the Australian title in 1934 and the ___ (7A) title in 1935. He also won many doubles and mixed-doubles titles. His Davis Cup record was outstanding – in twenty ties he lost ___ (13A) seven out of fifty-two matches. He was never ___ (16D) than when he was playing tennis and his successes ___ (23A) him the ___ (21D) of the British public, who ___ (16A) him in high esteem.

In 1936 he turned professional. Two years ___ (4D) he became an American citizen, serving in the US Air Force during the Second World War. When the war was ___ (8A), he set up a sportswear company which achieved good ___ (3A) and became highly successful.

He was ___ (9A) to be heard on sports broadcasts and was a member of the BBC radio team at Wimbledon for forty years. In 1984, a statue of him was unveiled at Wimbledon. He died in 1995.

See answer 203

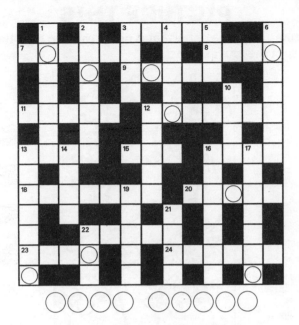

# TRILINES

Can you draw three straight lines from one edge to another, dividing the box into five parts with each section containing two different symbols?

See answer 203

# PICTURE THIS

Each picture contains a detail that is not present in the other three. Can you spot the four extra details?

# TAKE FIVE

The three answers in this mini-crossword read the same across and down. We've given you clues to the three words, but NOT in the right order. See how quickly you can solve it.

**1** Rage

**2** Opposite of south

**3** Particle of sand

See answer 204

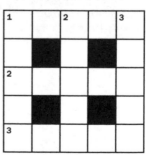

# WHAT'S MISSING?

Each picture is missing a detail that is present in the other seven.
Can you spot all eight missing details?

*See answer 204*

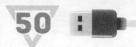

# TWO-TIMER

Two sets of clues to the same answers. Cryptic clues below and straight clues beneath the grid.

## ACROSS

6 Like two similar strikers (4-7)

8 Some slowcoaches are depressed (3)

9 Very small portion of sweetmeat (3)

10 Bird indicating canine happiness (7)

12 I had one to replace the dolt (5)

13 Dead keen boy (5)

14 Make regular journeys to the fold (3)

16 Be amazed at the miracle (6)

17 More cunning toxophilite (6)

18 All right to include a tree (3)

20 In the raw fully naked, that's dreadful! (5)

22 Virtuous sort of support is psychological (5)

23 It's a big blow in the China Seas and West Pacific (7)

24 No odd goings-on in this boat! (3)

26 One champion (3)

27 Do take steps after a meal (6-5)

## DOWN

1 Form of worship (3)

2 Not sink moving aloft (5)

3 Light-coloured petals dispersed (6)

4 Bill to deliver bitter (5)

5 Some housewives getting stitch (3)

6 Literally exchange a brief conversation (4,3,4)

7 Release, hand over broken cane (11)

10 Print of timber chopped up (7)

11 Understand the door is locked (5,2)

14 In favour of support for the most part (3)

15 Kay moved the beast (3)

19 Stick broken head on again (6)

21 Being dishonest at length (5)

22 Ivory grinder? (5)

25 Kelvin and I quietly have short sleep (3)

26 One caught part of play (3)

## ACROSS

**6** Compatible (4-7)

**8** Moo (3)

**9** Tiny (3)

**10** Bird (7)

**12** Foolish person (5)

**13** Patron saint of Wales (5)

**14** Work steadily at (3)

**16** Marvel (6)

**17** Bowman (6)

**18** Acorn tree (3)

**20** Very bad (5)

**22** Ethical (5)

**23** Asian hurricane (7)

**24** Ararat boat (3)

**26** Top card (3)

**27** Social occasion (6-5)

## DOWN

**1** Church seat (3)

**2** Stay up in the air (5)

**3** Type of crayon (6)

**4** Pungent (5)

**5** Use a needle and thread (3)

**6** Verbatim (4,3,4)

**7** Liberation (11)

**10** Engraved design (7)

**11** Finally grasp (5,2)

**14** For (3)

**15** Ox (3)

**19** Hold fast (6)

**21** Prone (5)

**22** Tooth (5)

**25** Nap (3)

**26** Parliamentary law (3)

*See answer 204*

# SKELETON CROSSWORD

Have double the fun with this puzzle: you've got to fill in the answers and the black squares! We've given you the bare bones to start and it will help you to know that the black squares in the finished grid form a symmetrical pattern, so that every black square has at least one other corresponding black square.

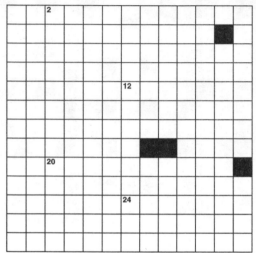

**ACROSS**

1 Overpriced
4 Skiing discipline
9 Smacked heavily
10 Bodily constriction between the ribs and hips
11 Work
12 Kitchen appliance which liquidises soups
14 Amateur
16 Lend a hand
19 Countersign
21 Be miserable
23 Jewelled coronet
24 Sweetener
25 Annually
26 Hoax

**DOWN**

1 Hooded robe
2 Acutely
3 Scenic ponds
5 Disobedient, uncontrolled
6 Estate owner in Scotland
7 Full development
8 Sun-dried brick
13 Smoothly
15 Letters for abroad
17 Entreat
18 Brief and abrupt
20 Histrionic scene
21 Proverbial centre
22 Additional tax

See answer 204

# JIG-WORD

No clues – just pattern and answers – but can you fit them in?

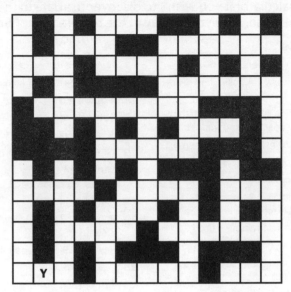

**3-letter words**
ADO
AIR
ALB
EVE
EYE
ODD
PET
PIE
PIN
RED

EASE
HILL
LOUD
OKRA
OPAL
PATE
PEST
PIER
POST
STUD
TERN

EVENT
TWINE

**6-letter words**
CURATE
ELICIT
ESCAPE
GOBLET
MANTLE
STROLL
TARTAN

**4-letter words**
AJAR
ALOE

**5-letter words**
APRON
ELATE

**8-letter word**
REPARTEE

*See answer 204*

# DATELINE

A number jig with a difference: with clues to figure out (with the help of a calculator if you wish!) to discover the date in the shaded line – in this case, a significant day in the recognition of bravery.

## ACROSS

1 Three-sevenths of 602

3 Reverse 1 Across, then divide by 4

5 Divide 33 Across by 63, then multiply by 4 squared

7 Freezing-point Fahrenheit

8 Cube root of 7880599

9 Roman CCCLXI

11 Multiply 7 Across by 11, subtract 7

13 Five-seventeenths of 2771

14 Multiply 27 Across by 518

16 Square 33 Across, subtract 35319

21 Inches in 1¾ miles

22 Minutes in a leap years's February

25 Four packs of cards plus three aces

27 Add the square root of 1369 to the square root of 5329

28 Number of Sherlock Holmes's house in Baker Street

30 Add the digits of 1 Across, then multiply by sum of digits of 1 Down

31 Triple 18, subtract three

32 Multiply the lives of a cat by 100

33 Square the former age of majority

34 Five-twenty-thirds of 1357

## DOWN

1 Number of inches in 63 yards

2 Multiply 7451 by 5 Across

4 A dozen baker's dozens

5 Outbreak of World War Two

6 Year of Prince Charles's birth

9 Cube 4 Down, subtract 5314

10 Multiply 24 Down by 28 Across, then add 6401

12 Old pence in £21

15 Pounds in 2 tons, 15 cwt and 7 stone

17 Reverse 19 Down, add 4495

18 Diamond plus golden anniversaries

19 Square 36, subtract 55

20 Ounces in 2688 stones

23 19 Down minus 11 squared

24 Subtract the first three digits of 26 Down from 50 gross

26 Divide 22 Across by 7 Across

29 8 per cent of 3300

*See answer 204*

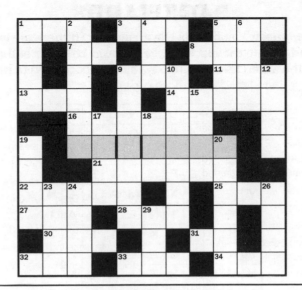

# MATCH UP

While putting the final touches to his work, the artist noticed that there were five discrepancies between his picture and the model. Can you spot them?

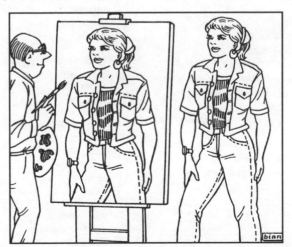

*See answer 205*

# BACKWARDS

For this puzzle, we've filled in the answers, but there are letters in the grid, where the black squares should be. You need to black out the unwanted letters to make a symmetrical grid to match the clues, which are listed in random order.

| S | P | A | D | D | E | N | D | A | I | L |
|---|---|---|---|---|---|---|---|---|---|---|
| A | L | T | A | R | A | O | U | I | J | A |
| T | O | O | M | I | T | T | E | D | A | D |
| A | L | L | E | P | R | E | T | E | W | E |
| Y | A | L | E | X | I | M | A | D | E | N |
| E | Y | E | L | I | N | E | R | A | A | I |
| S | E | E | K | A | K | A | T | E | L | L |
| E | R | A | N | G | E | L | E | A | D | O |
| N | O | S | O | R | T | I | N | G | N | U |
| O | P | E | R | A | E | N | E | E | D | S |
| R | E | D | E | B | A | T | E | R | O | E |

## ACROSS

- Relate
- Yemeni port
- Wants
- Hair preparation
- Left out
- Bother
- Sheep
- Arguer
- Supplementary items
- Before
- Large passenger-carrying vessel
- Classifying
- US university
- Seance board
- Church table
- Time
- Everyone
- Musical drama
- Search

## DOWN

- River barrier
- Short letter
- Moose
- Owing
- Seize
- Tier
- Linen for dressing wounds
- Skill
- Burdened
- Parasite
- Keen
- Open or wooded country
- Mineral
- Spicy dish
- Item of jewellery
- Born as
- Leak
- Coral reef
- Alleviated
- Spanish man
- Assisted

*See answer 205*

# JOLLY MIXTURES

In this puzzle, each clue is simply an anagram of the answer – but watch out! There might be more than one possible solution to each clue. For instance, the clue 'TALE' might lead to the answer 'LATE' or 'TEAL'. You'll have to look at how the answers fit into the grid to find out which alternative is correct.

**ACROSS**

1 TIME
5 GORE
8 STARE
10 ROMAN
11 TUBER
12 WEE
14 TORT
17 SATE
19 ARTICLE
20 PALE
21 CARE
22 CITADEL
23 RELY
25 VEER
28 TEA
30 GROAN
32 SUPER
33 VOILE
34 WOLF
35 MANE

**DOWN**

2 AMONG
3 RAT
4 WEST
5 ROB
6 OUTER
7 MUST
9 WENT
12 VALENCE
13 RATTEEN
15 EARLY
16 TREAD
17 LEAST
18 EAGER
23 POLO
24 LARGE
26 SERVE
27 FREE
29 RAID
31 OWN
32 APE

*See answer 205*

# CRYPTIC CROSSWORD

## ACROSS

1 Accident-prone tourist? (7)
5 Fool partly a comedian (7)
9 Decline to go with hoarder, a council worker (6,9)
10 Value of notability for the most part (5)
11 It is complicated to work out in detail (9)
12 Again guaranteed to have restored confidence (9)
14 Nothing in fog that is damp (5)
15 Wait at start of tennis match (5)
16 Headmistress fully content despite it being nerve-racking (9)
18 Near to said tea garment that can be worn in bed (9)
21 Deserve an order (5)
22 Male star-studded dinner? (10,5)
23 Cricket match and feature of it in practice (4,3)
24 Beat fellow on the line (7)

## DOWN

1 Thus without us, boatman becomes bowler (7)
2 Devilishly hot areas? (8,7)
3 Has to step for great speed (9)
4 Dog gets up before explosive gathering (5)
5 No end of gin hesitantly carried by Dutchman (9)
6 Strange, Leo, it will remain motionless (3,2)
7 Having a new feature – or a quarrel (4,1,10)
8 It pours from hill fissure (7)
13 Rosalind's found on open land in Ireland (9)
14 Strong-smelling substance on lemon pie or other fruit (4,5)
15 Smooth over mine to make play area (7)
17 Chattel turned out to be old shoe fastening (7)
19 Wildcat spotted by guide leader in the row (5)
20 N-note replacement music (5)

See answer 205

# STAIRCASE

When these Biblical characters are correctly placed along the horizontal rows, the letters in the diagonal staircase will spell out another one.

ABEL   ABSALOM   EPHRAIM

ESTHER   ISAAC   ISRAEL   NOAH

---

59

# DOT-TO-DOT

Join the dots from 1 to 30 to reveal the hidden picture.

*See answer 205*

# CROSSWORD

## ACROSS

4 Timber tree of the olive family (3)

8 Dot at the end of a sentence (4,4)

9 Regard as the same (6)

10 Composure (6)

11 Period between the beginning and end of a process (4,4)

13 Netherlands cheese (4)

15 Sulked, was miserable (5)

16 Money owed (4)

18 Bruise on the face (5,3)

20 Satanic creatures (6)

22 Writing-desk (6)

23 Form a barrier round (8)

24 Shell (peas) (3)

## DOWN

1 Shouldered (6)

2 Range of singing voice (4)

3 Butt (4)

4 Trick done with sheets (5-3,3)

5 Heavenly messenger (6)

6 Mated (of stags) (6)

7 Flower support (4)

12 Stuff your face (3)

13 Go back, as of the tide (3)

14 Take the ___, make fun of (6)

15 Gather together (4,2)

17 Ring for an arm or leg (6)

19 Hulking rough-mannered fellow (4)

20 Waterfowl (4)

21 Former German currency (4)

See answer 205

# KEYWORD

This puzzle has no clues in the conventional sense. Instead, every different number printed in the main grid represents a different letter (with the same number always representing the same letter, of course). For example, if 7 turns out to be a 'V', you can write in V wherever a square contains 7. We have completed a very small part of the puzzle to give you a start, but the rest is up to you.

| 16 | 2 | 4 | 18 | 16 | 11 | 10 | | 6 | 11 | 19 | 4 | 10 |
|----|----|----|----|----|----|----|----|----|----|----|----|----|
| 25 | | 25 | | 19 | | 13 | | 2 | | 12 | | 1 |
| 5 | 10 | 17 | 18 | 24 | | 19 | 4 | 17 | 16 | 10 | 24 | 10 |
| 8 | | 18 | | 12 | | 7 | | 9 | | 5 | | |
| 23 | 25 | 17 | 8 | 10 | 15 | 2 | 11 | | 15 | 11 | 19 | 10 |
| 9 | | | | 26 | | 17 | | 4 | | 25 | | 5 |
| 10 | 12 | 25 | 7 | 10 | 7 | | 20 | 25 A | 17 S | 21 P | 10 | 5 |
| 10 | | 24 | | 7 | | 17 | | 21 | | | | 19 |
| 11 | 25 | 8 | 9 | | 8 | 23 | 18 | 8 | 16 | 9 | 10 | 5 |
| | | 18 | | 15 | | 25 | | 18 | | 10 | | 11 |
| 10 | 24 | 3 | 2 | 18 | 5 | 26 | | 17 | 10 | 18 | 22 | 10 |
| 11 | | 2 | | 24 | | 10 | | 14 | | 5 | | 17 |
| 1 | 24 | 10 | 25 | 7 | | 7 | 10 | 17 | 18 | 17 | 8 | 17 |

A  B  C  D  E  F  G  H  I  J  K  L  M

N  O  P  Q  R  S  T  U  V  W  X  Y  Z

(The small grid is provided for ease of reference only)

| 1 | 2 | 3 | 4 | 5 | 6 | 7 | 8 | 9 | 10 | 11 | 12 | 13 |
|----|----|----|----|----|----|----|----|----|----|----|----|----|
| 14 | 15 | 16 | 17 | 18 | 19 | 20 | 21 | 22 | 23 | 24 | 25 | 26 |

*See answer 206*

# ADD-A-LETTER

Insert or add a letter to these four-letter words to make five-letter words which fit the rhyming clues. The six added letters should spell out a word.

| REAM | | Dairy product to top apple pie |
| GRAN | | Grumble, moan, gripe or sigh |
| LEAN | | Acquire knowledge, expand your brain |
| RISE | | Washing machine function, comes before 'drain' |
| SPIN | | Skeletal feature; the backbone |
| SATE | | Utter in a convincing tone |

# SMASHING

Four of the six shapes at the top can be found hidden in the picture. Can you work out which ones and where they are?

See answer 206

# SPIRAL

Every answer (except the first) uses the last letter of the preceding answer as its initial letter, the chain thus formed following a spiral path to the centre of the grid. The diagonals spell out the names of two ducks.

**START**

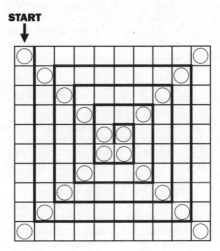

- Darling (7)
- Portable folding seat (9)
- Cavalier's opponent (9)
- Not easy (9)
- Meddle (6)
- Eraser (6)
- Scoundrel (6)
- Pedal (5)
- Mackintosh (8)
- Outburst (7)

- Scarf (7)
- Proportion (5)
- Past (4)
- Part of the eye (6)
- Unfriendly, detached (5)
- Excess flesh (4)
- People carrier (3)
- ___ Tuesday, pancake day (6)
- Slippery fish (4)
- Ocean (3)

*See answer 206*

# STORY CROSSWORD

Transfer the words which complete the story to the grid and then put the circled letters in the right order to discover the name of the famous person therein described.

On January 4th, 1809, a boy was born in Coupvray to a ___ (1D) and his wife. Even as a toddler, he liked to ___ (1A) in his father's work and was often to be found in his tack workshop.

One day, while his father was out of the workshop for a few ___ (13D), talking to a passing ___ (19D), the knife the little boy was using cut his eye. There was no ___ (23A) help available, so a ___ (21D) woman treated him with a herbal ___ (12A). Although she managed to staunch the flow of blood, the thing his parents ___ (8A) happened: he lost the sight of the injured eye. His other eye developed an infection, and two years ___ (10A) he became completely blind.

In 1814, Coupvray was invaded by Russian soldiers. He ___ (3D) their taunts and ill-treatment as they mocked him for his ___ (17D) ways. It was not long before the soldiers had managed to ___ (24A) his self-confidence and he scarcely went out of the house.

A year later, a new priest came to Coupvray. He found the boy bright and ___ (2D), and offered to become his teacher. Realising his pupil's potential, the priest arranged for him to go to the National Institute for Blind Youth in ___ (18A) Paris. In February 1819,

he became a ___ (15D) at the school. The Institute's teachers __ _ (25A) by fear. Boys who were slow and ___ (16D) at their lessons were given the ___ (9A). He ___ (14A) the rules and worked hard, even though he found the mindless ___ (4D) of the lessons hard to bear.

In 1821, a demonstration was given at the Institute of a system of 'night writing' which used dots and dashes punched into paper. He immediately started work to improve this system, and soon came up with a series of embossed dots which would ___ (20A) blind people to read at a ___ (7D) pace. Although his idea was as yet ___ (11A), the Head of the Institute prematurely introduced it to his pupils in a move which was to ___ (6D) the Governors and lead to the Head's dismissal.

Later, when he in turn became a ___ (4A) at the Institute, he secretly taught the children his new reading system, seeing it as an ___ (5D) to their learning.

In 1835, he contracted tuberculosis. It could not be ___ (18D), and he died from it on January 6th, 1852. Although his invention did not achieve recognition in his own lifetime, his system of dots is now highly __ _ (22A) by blind people everywhere.

See answer 206

# SMASHING

Can you see which four of these vases are exactly the same?

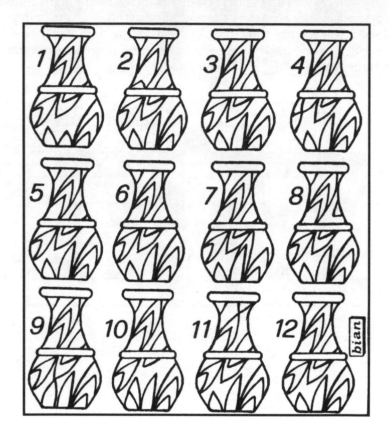

*See answer 206*

68

# WORDSEARCH

The 42 composers have all been hidden in the diagram. They have been printed across (backwards or forwards), or up or down, or diagonally, but always in a straight line without letters being skipped. You can use the letters in the diagram more than once. You will probably find it helpful to mark the words in the diagram and cross them off the list as you find them.

```
A T I B T Z F K S L L E W O H N
R H N E C A I O M W A L T O N E
N O I R H I N G A C S A M T V V
O M L N A B Z N I W H S R E G O
L S L S I W I L L I A M S O N H
D O E T K J O P L I N T K R B T
H N B E O H R Y I O T I O B L E
R C M I V E S E W O F D T B I E
T A A N S Y K S N I V A R T S B
L R C B K U W I A K B U A C S S
E L A H Y J D A H I C E B G C I
M I E Z M D A L G H H U R A M T
M S P W O A A N U N J T R T E N
U Z I H O M N N A S E L A B N E
H T E O B D W I V C A R G M O M
B E N E D I C T N T E L L X T E
C O R E L L I A T O Q K E Z T L
N T B U S O N I M K V A E L I C
```

| | | | |
|---|---|---|---|
| ARNOLD | BUSONI | IVES | RACHMANINOV |
| BACH | CILEA | JANACEK | SCARLATTI |
| BARTOK | CLEMENTI | JOPLIN | STRAVINSKY |
| BEETHOVEN | CORELLI | LAMBERT | TCHAIKOVSKY |
| BELLINI | ELGAR | LISZT | THOMSON |
| BENEDICT | FINZI | MACDOWELL | VAUGHAN |
| BERNSTEIN | GERSHWIN | MASCAGNI | WILLIAMS |
| BLISS | HODDINOTT | MATHIAS | WAGNER |
| BOITO | HOWELLS | MENOTTI | WALTON |
| BRUCH | HUMMEL | MOZART | WILLIAMSON |
| BRUCKNER | IBERT | NONO | |

See answer 206

# TINKER, TAILOR ...

To discover who this person is unscramble the words in the verse, which hints at what the person does. Write these words into the boxes below, reading across, and, if you've placed them in the correct order, the arrowed column will spell out the occupation.

He KROWS with
SKOBO and
HAPPLSTEM, too,

STRIPENTER
GANNIMES so that
you

Can DARE and
TUNNEDRADS
what's DAIS

In SAGGELUNA EVILA
and dead.

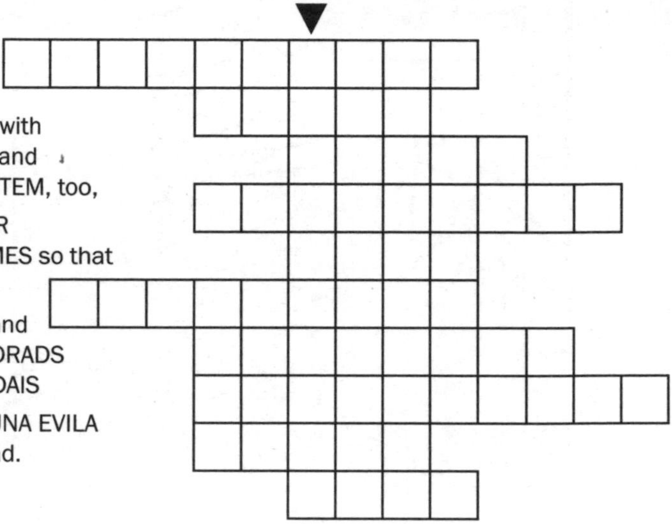

OCCUPATION: _____

See answer 206

# SILHOUETTE

Shade in every fragment containing a dot – and what have you got?

See answer 206

# CRYPTIC CROSSWORD

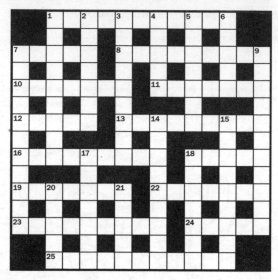

## ACROSS

1 It tells how aircraft may fly (11)
7 River god of a cold region (5)
8 I'd pass him crashing towards the centre of the vessel (9)
10 Going off back to team leader in the circle (7)
11 Came the revolution, used this weapon? (7)
12 It is clear that the apprentice is in agony (5)
13 Arthur Negus initially left behind strange traces of forefathers (9)
16 The Marines and I would otherwise have a month in France (9)
18 Frenchman keen for a giant (5)
19 Feature about bridge partners not having arrived in it (7)
22 Knock sailor returning two Cockney items of headwear (3-1-3)
23 Was guilty, having been sent to prison (9)
24 Trouble navy on deck (5)
25 Unprotected with a team of attackers? (11)

## DOWN

1 Uncomfortable, unwell and relaxing (3,2,4)
2 Alien involved in forge (7)
3 Type of action taken by railway worker back on top (9)
4 A few on the island giving the truth (5)
5 Fashionable groups of workers perhaps (7)
6 Innocent one enters the body of the church (5)
7 Precipitate action of a pedestrian (11)
9 Explain how the barn is illuminated? (4,5,2)
14 Case for an explosive vehicle on the hill (9)
15 This rogue could become virtuous (9)
17 Mother's pet dog (7)
18 The name concocted for an inflammable gas (7)
20 Directed me to help out (5)
21 Giant bird on a pole (5)

See answer 207

# NUMBER JIG

Just like a jig-word – but instead of letters, numbers.

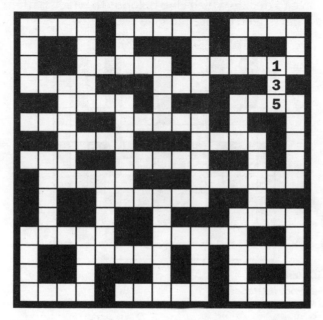

| **3-figures** | 1701 | **5-figures** | 81524 |
|---|---|---|---|
| 135 | 2198 | 11077 | 87174 |
| 214 | 2757 | 20617 | 90009 |
| 322 | 2881 | 29220 | 94685 |
| 402 | 3477 | 32220 | |
| 571 | 4567 | 34168 | **6-figures** |
| 782 | 5043 | 45678 | 187950 |
| 876 | 5871 | 45952 | 292424 |
| 986 | 6120 | 50613 | 403804 |
| | 7027 | 56789 | 551102 |
| **4-figures** | 7775 | 60408 | 626216 |
| 1211 | 8649 | 62127 | 701402 |
| 1234 | 9362 | 71142 | |
| 1357 | 9871 | 74748 | |

*See answer 207*

# DILEMMA

Two straightforward crosswords – but their clues have been mixed up. You have to decide which clue belongs to which pattern, but two words have been entered to give you a start.

The crossword grid contains the entered word **ERECT** at 18.

## ACROSS

| | |
|---|---|
| 1 Root vegetable | 1 Grasp |
| 5 Attack | 5 Old parish officer |
| 9 Core | 9 Frequently |
| 10 Untidy person | 10 Troublesome creatures |
| 11 Natural gift | 11 Scowl |
| 12 Bacon slice | 12 Walked unsteadily |
| 15 Unconscious | 15 Members of a boys' club |
| 17 Noise of disapproval | 17 Nevertheless |
| 18 Upright | 18 Deciduous conifer |
| 19 Pass away | 19 Devour |
| 20 Drink a small amount | 20 Become solid |
| 22 High temperature | 22 Theme |
| 24 Hive dweller | 24 Ancient |
| 26 Place of incarceration | 26 Drinking vessel |
| 27 Table attendant | 27 Benefactors |
| 28 Run after | 28 Scamp |
| 30 Bird of the dove family | 30 Hair covering the forehead |
| 31 Bestowed, granted | 31 Poem about the author's emotions |
| 32 Raised on one side | 32 Turn |
| 33 Buy back | 33 Ribbed |

**DOWN**

1 Secret
2 Tower
3 Chewy sweet
4 Farm bird
5 Implore
6 Fabric stiffener
7 Tree-lined road
8 Continent
13 Spooky
14 Sag
15 Wood fastener
16 Northern sea duck
20 Ghost
21 Colourful bird
22 Search for food
23 Compel
24 Rebound
25 Talked in a boring way
29 Organ of sight
30 Household animal

1 Pie topping
2 Disquiet
3 Cutting and shaping tool
4 Cancelled
5 Skill
6 Join the army
7 Began to grow light
8 Most recent
13 Carpenter's boring tool
14 Large black bird
15 Biting
16 Piece of furniture
20 Daze
21 Christmas glitter
22 Violent commotion
23 Gorge
24 Alternatives
25 Admire
29 Cover
30 Resinous tree

*See answer 207*

# KEYWORD

This puzzle has no clues in the conventional sense. Instead, every different number printed in the main grid represents a different letter (with the same number always representing the same letter, of course). For example, if 7 turns out to be a 'V', you can write in V wherever a square contains 7. We have completed a very small part of the puzzle to give you a start, but the rest is up to you.

| 8 | 10 | 24 | 9 | | 13 | 21 | 7 | 14 | 19 | 19 | 20 | 3 |
|---|---|---|---|---|---|---|---|---|---|---|---|---|
| 15 | | 10 | | 6 | | 15 | | 4 | | 3 | | 3 |
| 10 | 4 | 2 | 4 N | 9 O | 1 W | 4 | | 13 | 14 | 13 | 15 | 20 |
| 4 | | 3 | | 20 | | 24 | | 10 | | 3 | | 13 |
| 24 | 14 | 13 | 11 | 10 | 15 | 20 | 14 | 16 | 14 | 3 | 24 | |
| 14 | | | | 23 | | 3 | | 16 | | 21 | | 9 |
| 21 | 9 | 17 | 3 | 12 | 13 | | 22 | 3 | 23 | 18 | 25 | 7 |
| 3 | | 9 | | 10 | | 1 | | 7 | | | | 24 |
| | 14 | 4 | 12 | 9 | 5 | 14 | 21 | 15 | 12 | 14 | 9 | 4 |
| 14 | | 26 | | 10 | | 12 | | 19 | | 24 | | 15 |
| 19 | 15 | 7 | 2 | 13 | | 18 | 15 | 20 | 21 | 25 | 9 | 4 |
| 14 | | 3 | | 20 | | 14 | | 3 | | 20 | | 21 |
| 13 | 23 | 20 | 15 | 25 | 14 | 4 | 26 | | 26 | 20 | 10 | 3 |

**A B C D E F G H I J K L M**

**N O P Q R S T U V W X Y Z**

(The small grid is provided for ease of reference only)

| 1 | 2 | 3 | 4 | 5 | 6 | 7 | 8 | 9 | 10 | 11 | 12 | 13 |
|---|---|---|---|---|---|---|---|---|---|---|---|---|
| 14 | 15 | 16 | 17 | 18 | 19 | 20 | 21 | 22 | 23 | 24 | 25 | 26 |

*See answer 207*

# CROSSWORD

**ACROSS**

1 Person unable to sleep (9)
9 Fatness (7)
10 Electrically charged atom (3)
11 Arrest (3,2)
12 Mothballed (2,3)
14 Sliding trough (5)
16 Stick (5)
18 Small dog's bark (3)
19 Hard drinker (3)
21 Person who settles up (5)
22 Egg-shaped (5)
23 Sound forming a syllable (5)
25 Constructed (5)
26 Part of the lower body (3)
27 Piece of journalism (7)
28 Person who inflicts great pain and suffering (9)

**DOWN**

1 Stupid behaviour or action (6)
2 Ridicule (4,2)
3 World of trade (11)
4 Dishonourably (7)
5 Study (3)
6 Have a good look around (11)
7 Calf-length skirt (4)
8 Printed characters (4)
13 Aquatic bird of the rail family (4)
15 Indication of saintliness (4)
17 Small dog of various breeds used to hunt in burrows (7)
19 Scent bag (6)
20 Mood (6)
23 Calf's meat (4)
24 Escorted by (4)
25 Risk money on the outcome of an event (3)

*See answer 207*

# TWO-TIMER

Two sets of clues to the same answers. Cryptic clues below and straight clues beneath the grid.

## ACROSS

1 Whimsical quin at play (6)

5 Variety of nectar to cause a hypnotic state (6)

9 Ghostly eastern lake (5)

10 Decreased at home (6)

11 Vandalised pig pen found in the forest (6)

12 Of interest to consumers? (6)

15 Invisible passage for translation has not been prepared (6)

17 Bird to sway to and fro endlessly (3)

18 We must make an effort to do this ourselves (5)

19 Be very eager to have a small cube (3)

20 Broadcast so it can be heard (3)

22 What we do for the rest of the night (5)

24 Retiring from the cast (3)

26 On time to help an actor (6)

27 Weaken the Italian appearing in another duet (6)

28 Stern guide (6)

30 Two names for the beast (6)

31 Overturned counter at African port (5)

32 Four-foot cycle (6)

33 Ploughed a mowed field (6)

## DOWN

1 Case of the shakes (6)

2 Extremely small bomb? (6)

3 Provoke with a sharp instrument (6)

4 I leave new diet for him (3)

5 Unite most of the rank (3)

6 Feel sorry for the salesman with ten others (6)

7 Secured from Daniel (6)

8 Part of a car is English in England (6)

13 He gives Spaniard an alternative (5)

14 Was a junior officer shortly to get praise? (5)

15 Awfully rude about the note that incited (5)

16 A number had a meal, it is reported (5)

20 Courage for a ghost (6)

21 Dull court room (6)

22 Round field of activity (6)

23 Talk wildly about one, one who robs in the main (6)

24 Extracted what had been absorbed (6)

25 Dye that's liable to run! (6)

29 Run into a sheep (3)

30 Crowded mass on first June morning (3)

## ACROSS

1 Fanciful (6)
5 Stupor (6)
9 Creepy (5)
10 Pressed (6)
11 Forest in NE London (6)
12 Eatable (6)
15 Not noticed (6)
17 Legendary bird (3)
18 Strive (5)
19 Perish (3)
20 Female pig (3)
22 Slumber (5)
24 Bashful (3)
26 Without delay (6)
27 Add water (6)
28 Steering device (6)
30 Dog-like animal (6)
31 Moroccan port (5)
32 Bicycle for two (6)
33 Grassland (6)

## DOWN

1 Tremble (6)
2 Molecular (6)
3 Stylus (6)
4 Spread grass for drying (3)
5 Dead-heat (3)
6 Regret (6)
7 Pinned down (6)
8 Motor (6)
13 Contributor (5)
14 Extol (5)
15 Exhorted (5)
16 Rowing crew (5)
20 Alcoholic drink (6)
21 Lacking animation (6)
22 Globe (6)
23 Sea-robber (6)
24 Drew into one's mouth (6)
25 Egg-yolk colour (6)
29 Tup (3)
30 Preserve (3)

See answer 208

# THAT BIT OF DIFFERENCE

There are eight differences between these two cartoons.
Can you spot them?

See answer 208

# COG-ITATE

Can you work out which two weights will rise, and which two will fall when the man turns the lever as shown?

*See answer 208*

# TWO-BY-TWO

Each word in a clue can be preceded by the same two letters to spell out another word. For instance INTER, LATE and TENT can be preceded by PA to make PAINTER, PALATE and PATENT. Can you solve the three clues below, then spell out the three pairs of letters to make a six-letter word?

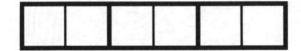

INK    RIFT    ROUGH

HEIST    ONE    TIRE

AIR    AMBER    URN

See answer 208

# PATHFINDER

Starting from the bold centre letter, move up or down or sideways (but NOT diagonally) to find the path through fifteen rulers and leaders.

| A | C | R | P | T | N | E | D | E | R | P |
|---|---|---|---|---|---|---|---|---|---|---|
| P | R | E | U | S | N | G | I | S | C | H |
| T | O | M | O | R | G | E | N | E | R | A |
| A | N | I | V | O | I | E | R | R | O | N |
| I | R | C | E | R | O | V | E | A | M | R |
| N | E | O | R | E | **S** | A | H | L | C | O |
| C | V | Y | M | P | C | N | C | I | H | T |
| O | O | G | E | R | E | I | N | E | T | A |
| M | M | A | N | O | L | A | T | F | C | I |
| C | R | E | D | T | L | C | H | R | M | D |
| O | N | D | U | C | O | R | A | I | A | N |

*See answer 208*

# STAIRCASE

When these foodstuffs are correctly placed along the horizontal rows, the letters in the diagonal staircase will spell out another one.

**BISCUIT**    **CHICKEN**    **CUSTARD**

**PANCAKE**    **RISSOLE**    **TAPIOCA**    **YOGHURT**

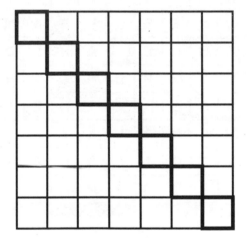

*See answer 208*

# JIG-WORD

No clues – just pattern and answers – but can you fit them in?

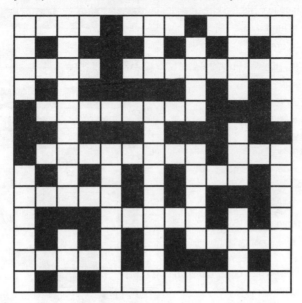

**3-letter words**

AFT
BYE
EAR
EBB
GOT
LET

**4-letter words**

COMA
COVE
FAWN
PATH

RUIN
VOTE
WREN

**5-letter words**

ARENA
EGRET
NIECE
OFFER
SHAPE
TRACE

**6-letter word**

FACTOR

**7-letter words**

MEASURE
ROOKERY

**8-letter words**

DORMOUSE
FORTIETH
NEGATIVE

**9-letter words**

EMERGENCY
EQUITABLE
METRONOME

See answer 208

# CROSSWORD

## ACROSS

1 Reduce in height (8)
6 Old armed soldier (9)
7 Great amount (3)
8 Secret political faction (5)
9 With no idea (8)
12 Nullify (4)
13 Male admirer (4)
16 Esteem for your own abilities (4-5)
18 Transport salesman (3,6)
19 Press (4)
20 Farmland unit (4)
23 Hypersensitive (8)
26 Moveable part of a helmet, that covers the face (5)
27 Garment often underwired (3)
28 Childminder (9)
29 Remote (8)

## DOWN

1 Appropriate (6)
2 Liable to change (9)
3 Squeezed together (8)
4 Quake (7)
5 Of the mouth (4)
10 Native of the warmer regions (10)
11 Inner division (10)
14 Sign up (5)
15 Sound of a bird (5)
17 Slow musical piece (5)
21 Recycled wood (9)
22 Domestic chimer (8)
24 Swell (7)
25 Striped (6)
26 Windmill blade (4)

*See answer 208*

# CROSSWORD

**ACROSS**

4 In the future (5)

9 Accomplish (7)

10 Throw out (of the premises) (5)

11 Affectionate name for grandma (3)

12 Ewe's mate (3)

13 Transient craze (3)

14 Reduce to ashes (7)

15 Large shop selling different kinds of goods (10,5)

19 Cough syrup (7)

20 Thick mat (3)

21 Plastic coat? (3)

22 View, look at (3)

23 Snap taken by a camera (5)

24 Reveal (secrets) (4,3)

25 Diaper (5)

**DOWN**

1 Loathing (6)

2 Pretence (4)

3 Series of small holes (11)

4 Give the use of for a time (4)

5 Airtight receptacle for processed foods (3,3)

6 Thing you need to make a vehicle move backwards (7,4)

7 Title given by foreigners to the emperor of Japan (6)

8 Eye ailment (4)

16 Wing, in poetry (6)

17 Blunder (4,2)

18 Arouse (6)

19 Run with long strides (4)

20 Depend confidently (4)

21 Arguable (point) (4)

*See answer 208*

# LETTER SET

All the letters needed for the answers in each row and column are given – cross-referencing coupled with anagram skills will ensure the correct solution. To get started, locate the rarer letters first.

| | |
|---|---|
| 1 AEGHNPRT | 1 AAEPSSTV |
| 2 AAEEORSS | 2 AEEIRRST |
| 3 AINNPTO | 3 BEEENOST |
| 4 ADEGLNNS | 4 ANORS |
| 5 EROTY | 5 AEGGHOPRY |
| 6 ABEHIRTV | 6 ELORT |
| 7 AAEEPRT | 7 AAAEISST |
| 8 EEEHLOST | 8 AEENNPTY |
| 9 AADESSSY | 9 ADDEHHLN |

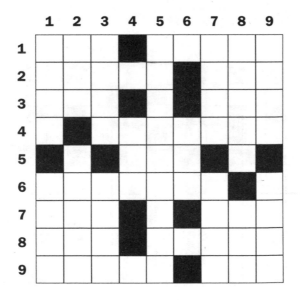

See answer 209

# ARROWORD

The arrows show the direction in which the answer to each clue should be placed.

| Cleopatra's killer | Uses a chair | ▼ | 20th Greek letter | ▼ | Play music for voluntary donations | ▼ | Permanent picture on the skin |
|---|---|---|---|---|---|---|---|
| ► | ▼ | | Salt Lake state ► / Drink cooler | | | | |
| Wife of Osiris in Egyptian myths ► | | | ▼ | | Jennifer Saunders' *Ab Fab* role | | Bypass, sidetrack |
| Admission vouchers ► | | | | | | | ▼ |
| ► | | | First musical note ► | | | | |
| Of Man or Dogs? | Available if needed (2,4) | | Type of industrial action (2-4) | Debt note (inits) ► | | | |
| ► | ▼ | | ▼ | 21st Greek letter | | Annoyed | |
| Dash, life | Geometrical painting style (2,3) ► | | ▼ | | | ▼ | |
| ► | | | | | Sir __ Hutton, cricketer | | East Anglian cathedral |
| Be quiet! | Industrial northern French city ► | | | | ▼ | | ▼ |
| ► | | | Estuary fish ► | | | | |
| (Put) in contact with (2,2) | Character in *Peter Pan* ► | | | | | | |

89

*See answer 209*

# GIANT CROSSWORD

**Across**

1 Musical group (9)
6 Lessened the strength of (8)
10 Travel across snow (3)
11 Pester (5)
12 Sedimentations (8)
13 Malady (7)
15 Stripe of contrasting colour (4)
17 Cold ___, ignore (8)
19 Sense of concern or curiosity (8)
21 Circle (4)
23 Triumph (7)
24 Unlearned (8)
27 Analysed (8)
30 Shattered, boken into pieces (7)
33 Buzz (3)
34 Long period of time (3)
35 Insistence (8)
36 Render capable for a task (7)
37 Distinctly (7)
39 Bitter (4)
40 Reinstate (7)
44 Feel of a surface (7)
47 Jointed appendage (4)
48 Make an effort (7)
50 Precisely (7)
51 Chance upon (8)
52 Pitch (3)
53 Wrath (3)
54 Believe to be true (7)
58 Supply that can be drawn on (8)
60 Distribute loosely (8)
62 Imaginary water nymph (7)
63 Let have for a limited time (4)
65 Covering for a letter (8)
66 Frozen dessert (3-5)
68 Medicine (4)
70 Tugging along behind (7)
74 Entrance way alarm (8)
75 Unit of weight (5)
76 Possess (3)
77 Lately (8)
78 Immensity (9)

**Down**

1 The tenth month of the year (7)
2 Series of linked objects (5)
3 Looked at (4)
4 Faucets (4)
5 The largest continent (4)
6 Broadest (6)
7 More or less (13)
8 Artist's tripod (5)
9 Damaged irreparably (9)
14 Extremely sharp or acute (7)
16 Fingers (6)
18 Kill by submerging in water (5)
20 Earth's nearest star (3)
22 Individual unit (4)
25 Embarrassed (7)
26 Mood (6)
28 Immediate (7)
29 At a previous point in time (7)
30 Pointed weapon (5)
31 Natives of Kuwait, eg (5)
32 Movement downward (7)
38 Alphabet characters (7)
41 Building (7)
42 Leaves prepared for smoking (7)
43 Non-professional (7)
45 Set free (5)
46 North African country (5)
48 Promotion of some product (13)
49 Conservatives (6)
55 Strange (7)
56 Stripped of rind or skin (6)
57 Abel's brother (4)
58 Oddment (9)
59 Dish out (5)
61 Dress-making aid (3)
64 Grades, stages (7)
65 Utilise (6)
67 Arch (5)
69 Gamut (5)
71 Lengthy (4)
72 Not in action (4)
73 Caprine animal (4)

See answer 209

# CREATURE FEATURE

All the clues in capital letters are anagrams of the names of creatures – those clues not in capital letters lead to normal solutions.

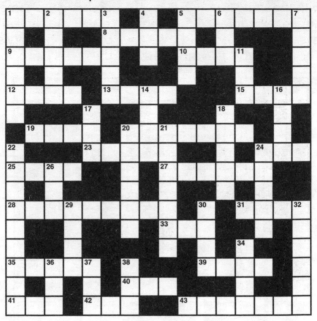

## Across

1 ALRSUW (6)
5 AELMPRY (7)
8 AEHNY (5)
9 Mollycoddle (6)
10 HMOT (4)
12 Slab of grass (4)
13 APSW (4)
15 AGOT (4)
19 AEFL (4)
20 ABCIORU (7)
23 AALKO (5)
24 Home for 40 Across (3)
25 ENOX (4)
27 CEGNTY (6)
28 AADILLMOR (9)
31 ABER (4)
33 LOW (3)
35 ADELN (5)
39 AGNT (4)
40 GIP (3)
41 ART (3)
42 EEW (3)
43 ACELOPT (7)

## Down

1 AIIPTW (6)
2 ELMRU (5)
3 EHRSW (5)
4 Animal doctor (3)
5 ABLM (4)
6 Got together (3)
7 Sailing vessel (5)
11 GHO (3)
14 AELS (4)
16 Mother's sister (4)
17 AKY (3)
18 DHNOU (5)
20 ACELTT (6)
21 ACCNOOR (7)
22 AABELOPRR (5,4)
24 EERST (5)
26 Forest tree (3)
29 Prayer ending (4)
30 GLSU (4)
32 ABBIRT (6)
34 AEHR (4)
36 Appropriate (3)
37 DEO (3)
38 AEP (3)

*See answer 209*

# KEYWORD

This puzzle has no clues in the conventional sense. Instead, every different number printed in the main grid represents a different letter (with the same number always representing the same letter, of course). For example, if 7 turns out to be a 'V', you can write in V wherever a square contains 7. We have completed a very small part of the puzzle to give you a start, but the rest is up to you.

| 17 | 6 | 20 | 15 |  | 9 | 17 | 2 | 14 | 20 | 18 | 1 | 19 |
|---|---|---|---|---|---|---|---|---|---|---|---|---|
| 18 |  | 18 |  | 11 |  | 19 |  | 13 |  | 20 |  | 5 |
| 12 | 19 | 4 | 5 | 18 | 21 | 19 |  | 16 | 18 | 20 | 17 | 19 |
| 12 |  | 5 |  | 17 |  | 17 |  | 18 |  | 19 |  | 4 |
| 24 | 19 | 18 | 21 | 10 | 14 | 18 | 4 | 1 | 19 | 4 | 17 |  |
| 6 |  |  |  | 14 |  | 22 |  | 24 |  | 7 |  | 7 |
| 4 | 19 | 19 | 15 | 19 | 21 |  | 26 | 9 | 22 | 25 | 19 | 4 |
| 19 |  | 8 |  | 4 R |  | 23 |  | 11 |  |  |  | 18 |
|  | 17 | 19 | 3 | 18 A | 7 | 19 | 13 | 18 | 4 | 6 | 18 | 13 |
| 2 |  | 2 |  | 21 D |  | 12 |  | 26 |  | 11 |  | 21 |
| 20 | 6 | 1 | 4 | 19 |  | 24 | 19 | 20 | 6 | 12 | 18 | 21 |
| 19 |  | 9 |  | 4 |  | 25 |  | 19 |  | 19 |  | 18 |
| 16 | 9 | 4 | 19 | 17 | 1 | 4 | 25 |  | 17 | 20 | 6 | 21 |

A B C D E F G H I J K L M
N O P Q R S T U V W X Y Z

(The small grid is provided for ease of reference only)

| 1 | 2 | 3 | 4 | 5 | 6 | 7 | 8 | 9 | 10 | 11 | 12 | 13 |
|---|---|---|---|---|---|---|---|---|---|---|---|---|
| 14 | 15 | 16 | 17 | 18 | 19 | 20 | 21 | 22 | 23 | 24 | 25 | 26 |

See answer 209

# PHOTO OPPORTUNITY

Which one of the nine photographs was taken by the photographer?

*See answer 209*

# ROUNDABOUT

Solutions to Radial clues (1 to 24) either start from the outer edge of the circle and read inwards, or start from the inner ring and read outwards to the edge (so they are all five-letter words). Solutions to Circular clues read in either a clockwise or an anticlockwise direction around the circle.

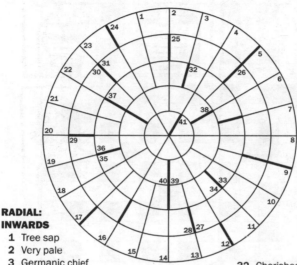

**RADIAL:**
**INWARDS**

1 Tree sap
2 Very pale
3 Germanic chief god
8 Spanish square
12 Javelin
15 Willow for baskets
18 Seashore
19 Sailor's cry
20 Right-hand page
24 Sewer

**OUTWARDS**

4 Masticates
5 Intone
6 Goddess of the harvest
7 Stringed instrument
9 Sky blue
10 Viper

11 Larry ___, harmonica player
13 Uplift
14 Sum up (abbrev)
16 Come to a point
17 Savour
21 Water animal
22 Make a speech
23 Planet's path

**CIRCULAR:**
**CLOCKWISE**

9 Go astray
25 Boar's mate
26 Little ___, Dickens character
28 Special branch of the forces (initials)
31 Anger

32 Cherished
34 Hawaiian garland
36 Deed
37 Put to shame
40 Orient
41 Cardboard container

**ANTICLOCKWISE**

4 Grassy expanse
8 Mail
16 Strong tying fibres
23 Row of houses
27 Lord of the realm
29 Cast a ballot
30 Golf peg
33 Two-way
35 Savoury jelly
38 Inheritor
39 Cutting tool

*See answer 209*

# MISSING LINKS

The answer to each clue is a word which has a link with each of the three words listed. This word may come at the end (eg Head linked with Beach, Big and Hammer), at the beginning (eg Black linked with Beauty, Board and Jack) or a mixture of the two (eg Stone linked with Hail, Lime and Wall).

**ACROSS**

6 Dial, Seeker, Trap (3)
8 Hostile, Natural, Working (11)
9 Bag, Time, Trade (3)
10 Action, Descendant, Route (6)
11 Circle, Conscious, Precious (4)
13 Belly, Luck, Plant (3)
14 Baby, Living, Russian (4)
15 Grand, Straw, Touch (5)
18 Field, Labour, Task (5)
19 Child, Nest, Puppy (4)
20 Art, Festival, Idol (3)
23 First, Fixed, Going (4)
24 Flag, Shop, Unit (6)
26 Lift, Lodge, Slope (3)
28 Lock, Oven, Winning (11)
29 Detector, Down, White (3)

**DOWN**

1 Boy, Count, Hunter (4)
2 Control, Length, Responsibility (7)
3 Air, House, Wall (5)
4 Day, Liner, Off (3)
5 Director, Major, Strike (7)
6 Comic, Lighting, Search (5)
7 Attitude, Effect, Equity (8)
12 Football, Fork, Perfect (5)
14 Bomb, Instructions, Waste (8)
16 Drama, Jewellery, National (7)
17 Chamber, Privy, Town (7)
21 Asking, Cut, War (5)
22 Mail, Navy, Pardon (5)
25 Binder, Finger, Tone (4)
27 Drum, Essential, Lamp (3)

See answer 210

# CROSSWORD

**ACROSS**

1 Film based on the life of a famous person (6)

5 Infectious (of a tune) (6)

9 Single unit (3)

11 Space to stretch out (7)

12 Park wardens (7)

13 Having a non-gloss finish (4)

15 Put your foot down heavily (5)

16 Livery (4)

17 Agreeable (4)

19 Soft and fluffy, feathery (5)

20 Bathing beach or open-air swimming pool (4)

24 Dream-like (7)

25 Experienced performer (3,4)

26 World's second-largest bird (3)

27 Container that tips out its contents at the bottom (6)

28 Temporarily lose control and let fury take over (3,3)

**DOWN**

2 Bullion bar (5)

3 High deck astern (4)

4 Financial supervisor (11)

5 Dignified, grand (11)

6 Very small (4)

7 Animal associated with laughing (5)

8 Tendency to fat (9)

10 Whitish (hair) (3,6)

14 End of the foot (3)

16 Solidify (3)

18 Rare object (5)

21 Very cross (5)

22 Pry (4)

23 Fringe (4)

*See answer 210*

# DILEMMA

Two straightforward crosswords – but their clues have been mixed up. You have to decide which clue belongs to which pattern, but two words have been entered to give you a start.

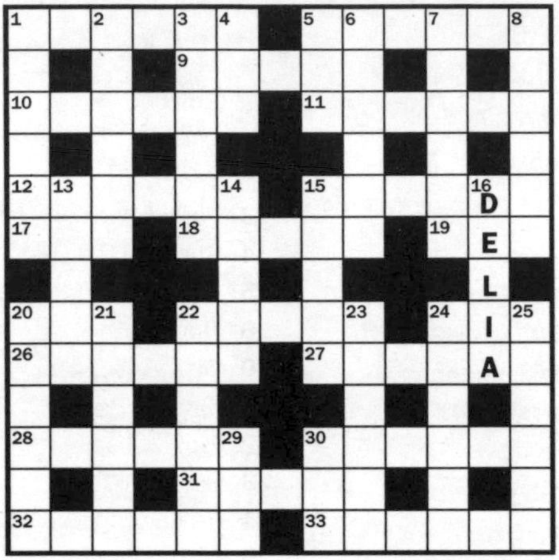

The crossword grid contains the letters D, E, L, I, A spelling "DELIA" vertically at position 16.

## ACROSS

| | | | |
|---|---|---|---|
| 1 | Hot drink | 1 | Shrill cry of fear |
| 5 | Barked sharply | 5 | Entertained |
| 9 | Bread-maker | 9 | Tusk material |
| 10 | Wine jug | 10 | Brawl |
| 11 | Task | 11 | Weighing device |
| 12 | Young angel | 12 | Lumpy, rugged |
| 15 | Front of a building | 15 | Harmless |
| 17 | That woman | 17 | Knight's title |
| 18 | Took things easy | 18 | Sweetener |
| 19 | Delve | 19 | Resting place |
| 20 | Constricting snake | 20 | Rider Haggard novel |
| 22 | Doze, slumber | 22 | Artist's stand |
| 24 | Drink daintily | 24 | Explosive (inits) |
| 26 | Person with a drug habit | 26 | Be present (at) |
| 27 | Rogue | 27 | Permissiveness, licence |
| 28 | Cutting implements | 28 | Posted |
| 30 | Popular fruit | 30 | Unusual object |
| 31 | Sorcery | 31 | Church walkway |
| 32 | Expanse of arid land | 32 | Required |
| 33 | Beat | 33 | Cloth dealer |

## DOWN

1. Laundry stiffener
2. Roof timber
3. ___ Tower, Parisian landmark
4. Adam's partner
5. Word of agreement
6. Any immense number
7. Wan
8. Giving medicine to
13. Biblical king
14. River nymph
15. Ring-shaped roll
16. ___ Smith, TV cook
20. Gotham City superhero
21. Look up to
22. Make popular
23. Royal residence
24. Angry outburst
25. Member of a sporting side
29. Parent
30. Auction offer

1. Spiny plant
2. Agricultural worker
3. Counting device
4. Spring month
5. Metric land measure
6. Bowman
7. Ancient Egyptian sacred beetle
8. Evaded
13. Period of darkness
14. Constructed
15. High temperature
16. Huge man
20. Dismissed, fired
21. Moral philosophy
22. Plot, conspire
23. Run in tights
24. Be sparing
25. Dictator
29. Use a chair
30. Aged

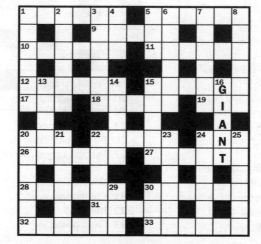

*See answer 210*

# CROSSWORD

### ACROSS

1. Steak (1-4)
5. Blast of a horn (4)
6. Assessor (6)
7. Span (4)
8. Swelling on the toe (6)
9. Tablet you drop in the tub (4,4)
12. Flying craft (9)
15. Complain, pester (3)
16. TV studio sign (2,3)
17. Small seed (5)
18. Is able (3)
19. On each occasion (5,4)
21. Cannibal (3-5)
24. In a mess (6)
25. Cereal by-product (4)
26. Stick of coloured wax for drawing (6)
27. Single time (4)
28. Condition (5)

### DOWN

2. Great technical skill or brilliance (7)
3. Sustain (7)
4. Brief (7)
5. Unruffled (8)
9. Mental ability (10)
10. Instrument used to measure air pressure (4,5)
11. Compared with the last twelve months (4-2-4)
13. Descendants (7)
14. Revolutionary (9)
20. Abjure (8)
21. Nomad (7)
22. Entice (7)
23. Furthest, last (7)

*See answer 210*

# JIG-WORD

No clues – just pattern and answers – but can you fit them in?

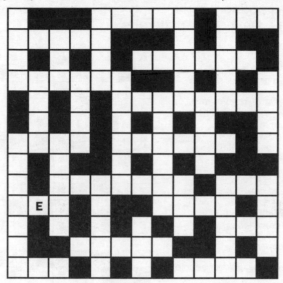

| 3-letter words | DAUB | 6-letter words |
|---|---|---|
| BAG | DOOR | BALDER |
| EEL | OMEN | DIATOM |
| EGG | RATE | REDDEN |
| ELL | ROSE | TEASER |
| NIL | | WARMLY |
| ROT | | |
| TEA | **5-letter words** | |
| URN | ARENA | |
| | BELIE | **7-letter words** |
| **4-letter words** | CABLE | ADVERSE |
| ABLE | DECRY | BLENDER |
| AFAR | EASEL | |
| ARCH | LARGO | |
| CREW | REGAL | **8-letter word** |
| DASH | TENSE | ECTODERM |

*See answer 210*

# PIECEWORD

With the help of the Across clues only, can you fit the 35 pieces into their correct positions in the empty grid (which, when completed, will exhibit a symmetrical pattern)?

**ACROSS**

1 South American country

2 Woodwind instrument; squeeze

3 Coffer; coil of yarn

4 Lawn scraper; hickory nut; immense

5 Animal den; Dutch cheese

6 Encounter; fragrance; lecherous look

7 Lukewarm

8 Edge along; golden treacle

9 Long hair curl

10 Savage; gangway

11 Act on stage

12 Insect grub; Indian corn

13 Emit rays

14 Verse; stiff

15 Muffler

16 Group of cattle; wigwam; unattached

17 Ninth Greek letter; lazy

18 German city; wash; highest male voice

19 Serpent; condition

20 Step; be aware of

21 Reject

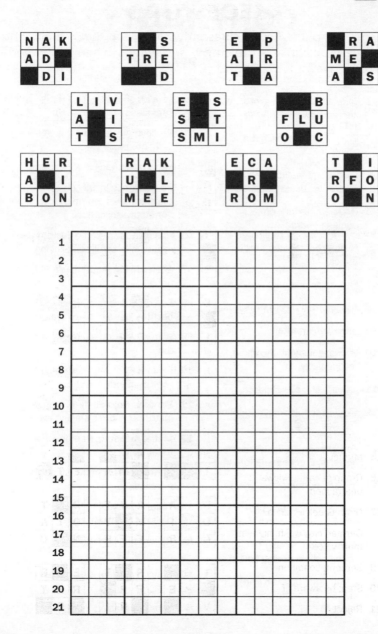

| N | A | K |
|---|---|---|
| A | D | ■ |
| ■ | D | I |

| I | ■ | S |
|---|---|---|
| T | R | E |
| ■ | ■ | D |

| E | ■ | P |
|---|---|---|
| A | I | R |
| T | ■ | A |

| ■ | R | A |
|---|---|---|
| M | E | ■ |
| A | ■ | S |

| L | I | V |
|---|---|---|
| A | ■ | I |
| T | ■ | S |

| E | ■ | S |
|---|---|---|
| S | ■ | T |
| S | M | I |

| ■ | ■ | B |
|---|---|---|
| F | L | U |
| O | ■ | C |

| H | E | R |
|---|---|---|
| A | ■ | I |
| B | O | N |

| R | A | K |
|---|---|---|
| U | ■ | L |
| M | E | E |

| E | C | A |
|---|---|---|
| ■ | R | ■ |
| R | O | M |

| T | ■ | I |
|---|---|---|
| R | F | O |
| O | ■ | N |

(grid numbered 1–21)

 103

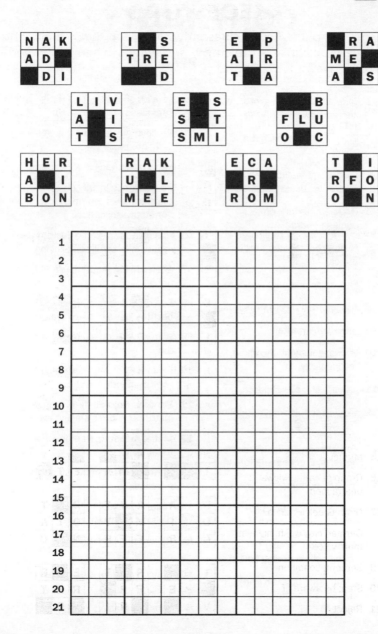

*See answer 210*

# CONTINUITY

No black squares – heavy bars mark the ends of words.

## ACROSS

1 1582 time change (9,8)

2 Take away; close; Egypt's river; kitchen stove

3 Eternal; ogre; supernatural being

4 Sell; parrot-fashion learning; reverence; deserter; stitch

5 Finished; peruse; dregs; duelling sword

6 Pebble; cure leather; tatter; attack

7 Fish eagle; hesitate; indicate

8 Accustom; ethical; citrus fruit

9 Introductory; fatal

10 Placid; dispatch; uncooked; recline lazily

11 Agent's fee; overshadow

12 Sloping script; upright; public speaker

13 Fork prong; ___ lights, aurora borealis; European nationality

14 Imperil; portent; wander off

15 Young deer; smear; two-wheeled vehicle; limb

16 Trade union; mother's ruin; young eel; deafening sound

17 Lower limb; build an annex; clarinet's mouthpiece; army canteen

## DOWN

1 Serious; detergent; malicious

2 London shopping road (6,6); senseless

3 Remove errors from; choose; task; hairpiece

4 Important principle (6,4); purify

5 Six deliveries in cricket; Chester's river; number in a nonet; tavern; carton

6 Holiday town; Middle-Eastern republic; forcefully convincing

7 Alternatively; gentleman's title; brink

8 Sea off Greece; charged particle; head of corn; coach

9 Water nymph; peculiar; hunting dog

10 Swimming stroke; burn slightly; twelfth month

11 Princess Royal; before; stringed instrument; boy's singing voice

12 Metric measure; fragrance; plot together

13 Sprite; serpent; move stealthily; hazarded

14 Tidier; rowing blade; fibber; division of school year

15 Raised platform; ache; spinning toy; rant

16 Concurring; too; Indian dresses

17 Sunbeam; marry; vote counter; songs of praise

*See answer 211*

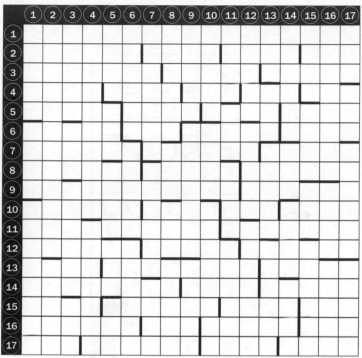

# RIDDLE ME REE

My first is in SHIVER and also in SHAKE,

My second's in ICING not in FLAKE,

My third's in both BLIZZARD and BLOW,

My fourth's in SLEET though not in SNOW,

My fifth's in GLACIER and also FREEZE,

My sixth is in CHILBLAINS but not in SNEEZE,

My seventh's in ARCTIC but not in WINTRY,

My whole is a very cold place indeed to be.

See answer 211

# SUM-UP

Using the totals given, can you calculate the price of each banana, orange, apple and pear?

# 4-SQUARE

Solve these four clues and then rearrange the solutions into a sixteen-letter phrase, for which a clue is given. The two diagonals also make four-letter words.

PANS

A FEW

OTTER'S DEN

DONATED

Clue: Shift a footballer's target (4,3,9)

See answer 211

# KEYWORD

This puzzle has no clues in the conventional sense. Instead, every different number printed in the main grid represents a different letter (with the same number always representing the same letter, of course). For example, if 7 turns out to be a 'V', you can write in V wherever a square contains 7. We have completed a very small part of the puzzle to give you a start, but the rest is up to you.

| 21 | 25 | 9 | 10 | 2 | 17 | | 7 | 13 | 2 | 10 | 11 | 15 |
|---|---|---|---|---|---|---|---|---|---|---|---|---|
| 25 | | 10 | | 22 | 12 | 8 | 21 | 10 | | 19 | | 6 |
| 9 | 10 | 22 | 18 | 12 | 20 | | 2 | 18 | 12 | 11 | 6 | 9 |
| 6 | | 6 | | 25 | 18 | 20 | 12 | 9 | | 18 | | 7 |
| 3 | 18 | 9 | 25 | | 11 | 18 | 19 | | 20 | 12 | 26 | 18 |
| 10 | 16 | 17 | 6 | 11 | | 7 | | 22 P | 10 | 9 | 12 | 11 |
| | 12 | | 17 | 12 | 23 | | 1 | 18 A | 22 | | 19 | |
| 7 | 6 | 22 | 10 | 20 | | 4 | | 17 T | 6 | 25 | 18 | 11 |
| 18 | 7 | 12 | 20 | | 2 | 18 | 19 | | 17 | 6 | 9 | 10 |
| 20 | | 10 | | 17 | 24 | 9 | 6 | 5 | | 26 | | 25 |
| 19 | 6 | 9 | 25 | 10 | 18 | | 3 | 6 | 16 | 12 | 25 | 23 |
| 18 | | 19 | | 2 | 14 | 12 | 9 | 11 | | 19 | | 17 |
| 22 | 11 | 10 | 25 | 17 | 13 | | 18 | 15 | 9 | 10 | 2 | 24 |

## A B C D E F G H I J K L M
## N O P Q R S T U V W X Y Z

(The small grid is provided for ease of reference only)

| 1 | 2 | 3 | 4 | 5 | 6 | 7 | 8 | 9 | 10 | 11 | 12 | 13 |
|---|---|---|---|---|---|---|---|---|---|---|---|---|
| 14 | 15 | 16 | 17 | 18 | 19 | 20 | 21 | 22 | 23 | 24 | 25 | 26 |

*See answer 211*

# STORY CROSSWORD

Transfer the words which complete the story to the grid and then put the circled letters in the right order to discover the name of the famous person therein described.

The ___ (12A) of a general and the grandson of a nobleman who had settled in Santo ___ (22A), he was born in France in 1802. He had little formal education but found work as a clerk to the duke of Orléans in Paris. Here he became an enthusiastic reader, particularly enjoying ___ (4D) stories set in the 16th and 17th ___ (11D).

While working for the duke, he attended a performance by an English Shakespearean company, an ___ (8A) which inspired him to try to ___ (2D) plays. His play *Henry III and His ___* (15A) was performed by the Comedie Francaise in 1829. A year ___ (19A) the same company produced his romantic drama, *Christine*.

He considered writing an ___ (6A) career and, over the ___ (13A) few years, he went on to write more plays including *The Tower of Nesle*, *Catherine ___* (1A) and *The Alchemist*. He wrote a huge number of novels, too, many of them ___ (1D). His best-known works are *The ___* (14A) *Musketeers* and *The Count of ___* (18D)-*Cristo*, which both appeared in 1844. They were translated into English in 1846. ___ (23A) of both of these books were ___ (9D).

His writing earned him a fortune, and he adopted an extravagant ___ (12D) of life. He was an intelligent ___ (18A) and he soon realised that he would be able to earn more money if he could produce books more quickly. He dreamt up a ___ (5D) that would help him to achieve this aim and began to employ a ___ (21D) of ___ (7A) writers who penned books for him. This enabled him to bring out about 1,200 novels under his name, a scheme which earned him enormous amounts of money.

He ran an estate near Paris where he lived like a ___ (16A). He ___ (20D) bought many works of art and set up a variety of businesses, though most made large financial losses. Their failure forced him to ___ (17A) a considerable amount of his earnings to cover business liabilities. In addition, he supported numerous ___ (24A), one of whom was the mother of his son who grew up to become a writer, too.

He ___ (3D) in 1870 at the age of sixty-eight, by which time his extravagance had brought him to the brink of bankruptcy. Some of his books are still in print today and he is considered ___ (10A) of France's finest writers of the Romantic Period.

*See answer 211*

# BOXWISE

Put these three-letter groups into the twelve numbered boxes to produce twelve six-letter words, each of which starts in one box and finishes in another as indicated by an arrow. For instance, 2 and 5 make a six-letter word, but not 5 and 9. One group has been filled in to start you off.

ATE  DER  EST  GOS

~~HON~~  MIT  PEL  PER

PRO  SEN  SIP  TEN

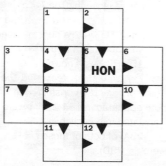

See answer 211

# CROSSWORD

**ACROSS**

1 State of neglect (9)
9 Learned institution (7)
10 Betting suggestion (3)
11 Massive person (5)
12 Long hilltop (5)
14 Breed of dog favoured by the Queen (5)
16 Exuberant enjoyment, zest (5)
18 Centre of a wheel (3)
19 Provide weapons to (3)
21 Hot and damp, as of weather (5)
22 Eskimo snow-hut (5)
23 Downright (5)
25 Passed on to another tenant (5)
26 Idiot (3)
27 Stand-off (7)
28 Edict (9)

**DOWN**

1 Sever (6)
2 Wonderful (6)
3 UK flower? (7,4)
4 Mixture of diverse elements (7)
5 Brown rodent (3)
6 Relating to a diet thought to promote well-being and longevity (11)
7 Ward (off) (4)
8 Rubber wheel-covering (4)
13 Banking system (4)
15 Depose (4)
17 Maker of seats for horse riders (7)
19 Non-acidic substance (6)
20 Hair application (6)
23 Military division (4)
24 Summits (4)
25 Communist colour (3)

*See answer 211*

# TINKER, TAILOR ...

To discover who these people are unscramble the words in the verse, which hints at what they do or have done. Write these words into the boxes below, reading across, and, if you've placed them in the correct order, the arrowed column will spell out the occupation.

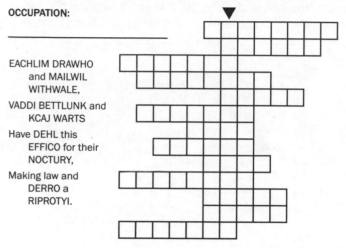

**OCCUPATION:**
_____

EACHLIM DRAWHO and MAILWIL WITHWALE,

VADDI BETTLUNK and KCAJ WARTS

Have DEHL this EFFICO for their NOCTURY,

Making law and DERRO a RIPROTYI.

# SILHOUETTE

Shade in every fragment containing a dot – and what have you got?

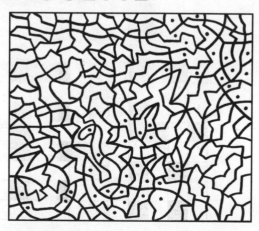

*See answer 211*

# WORDSEARCH

The 39 different kinds of aircraft have all been hidden in the diagram. They have been printed across (backwards or forwards), or up or down, or diagonally, but always in a straight line without letters being skipped. You can use the letters in the diagram more than once. You will probably find it helpful to mark the words in the diagram and cross them off the list as you find them.

```
V I S C O U N T H P E N C M X V
R R C D A K O T A L V O T J I G
M E V O D K O U G E N T R K L G
O T D Q N M H A G C L G I A R V
H N N R S E A O T R N D O B C
A U M E A N T R R A G I E T C B
W H G B E M D E U R A L N I A R
K I W D L E A G L T I L T U N I
T W L R L E A L O L R E H Q B T
Y O A G E J N R A O A W R S E A
G D S H V K E H T S B T A O R N
S K Y H A W K C E O I M I M R N
F S A B R E E O Z I D O U O A I
A R A V A V S P F X M A J J N A
T E M O C T L O B R E D N U H T
K I T T Y H A W K K E G A R I M
M E R L I N I H S U Y L I U O Q
L E K N I E H N O C L A F L R T
```

ARAVA

BLENHEIM

BRITANNIA

CANBERRA

CARAVELLE

COMET

CONCORDE

CONSTELLATION

DAKOTA

DOVE

FALCON

FOKKER

GLADIATOR

GOLDEN EAGLE

HARRIER

HEINKEL

HUNTER

ILYUSHIN

JAGUAR

JUMBO

KITTY HAWK

MERLIN

MIG

MIRAGE

MOHAWK

MOSQUITO

SABRE

SALAMANDER

SEAHAWK

SKYHAWK

THUNDERBOLT

TIGER MOTH

TORNADO

TRIDENT

VECTOR

VEGA

VIKING

VISCOUNT

WELLINGTON

*See answer 112*

# NUMBER JIG

Just like a Jig-word – but instead of letters, numbers.

| **3-figures** | 5460 | **6-figures** | **7-figures** |
|---|---|---|---|
| 209 | 6325 | 146640 | 2336540 |
| 253 | 6632 | 298017 | 3231183 |
| 392 | 7340 | 299163 | 3410601 |
| 418 | 8033 | 305621 | 4316299 |
| 423 | 9057 | 376418 | 5401012 |
| 873 | | 419382 | 8432199 |
| 911 | | 431701 | 9530373 |
| | **5-figures** | 571206 | |
| **4-figures** | 13623 | 650279 | |
| 1132 | 20223 | 763041 | |
| 2575 | 35221 | 842077 | |
| 2650 | 69676 | 925717 | |
| 3308 | 93284 | 972926 | |

*See answer 112*

# BRACER

The first part of each clue gives a six-letter answer, five of whose letters make up the five-letter answers to the second part and four of which make up the four-letter answer to the third part. The unused letter from the first answer is entered into column A, and that from the second answer into column B. The two columns when completed, spell out the names of two ballet dancers.

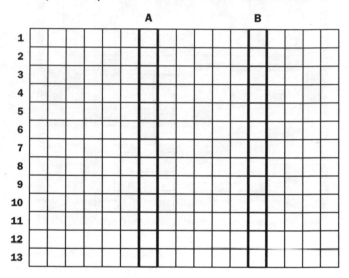

1  Young girl; excavated; eat supper

2  Indication; profits; serenade

3  Esteem; reverie; honey drink

4  Strong-smelling bulb; Holy ___, cherished goal; deceiver

5  Far East; cosmetic lotion; torn

6  Do again; Princess Anne's son; member of the nobility

7  Solemn, official; plant-life; by mouth

8  Waterproof jacket; holy book; grade

9  Hire charge; tilted; overdue

10  Cavalier; end of day; nearby

11  Hi-fi; guide; remainder

12  Carry; rabbit-skin; ice-cream holder

13  Sailor; minister's home; sewn edge

*See answer 212*

# SPIRAL

Every answer (except the first) uses the last letter of the preceding answer as its initial letter, the chain thus formed following a spiral path to the centre of the grid. The diagonals spell two drinks.

**START**

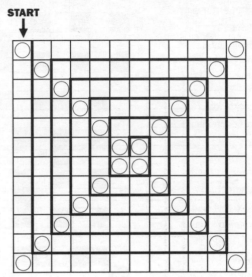

- Disney character (6,5)
- Soil (5)
- The Netherlands (7)
- Small rodent (8)
- Female ruler (7)
- Robert Burns' country (8)
- Tooth doctor (7)
- Venomous spider (9)
- Huge ocean (8)
- Whitehall monument (8)
- Tirade, lecture (8)
- "___ my dear Watson" – Sherlock Holmes saying (10)
- Cowardly colour (6)

- Charles, Prince of ___ (5)
- Long thin dagger (8)
- Fruit garden (7)
- Spanish chaperone (6)
- Operatic song (4)
- Come into view (6)
- Niche (6)
- Spanish wine punch (7)
- ___ and Crafts, movement (4)
- Quick gulp of drink (4)
- Clothing (4)
- Sheep's noise (3)
- Swiss mountain (3)

 115

*See answer 212*

# CROSSWORD

**ACROSS**

1 Detonate (2,3)

5 See the sights (4)

6 Summertime star sign (6)

7 Altercations (4)

8 Complete in natural development (6)

9 Hair at the front of the head (8)

12 Sedimentary rock (9)

15 Body part containing a lobe (3)

16 Olympic stadium (5)

17 Landowner (5)

18 Whitish timber (3)

19 Decorative roof slab (5,4)

21 Pass judgement on (8)

24 Unfledged (6)

25 Tiny skirt (4)

26 Share (6)

27 Horrible (4)

28 Unmoving (5)

**DOWN**

2 Culinary herb (7)

3 Breakdown (7)

4 Rampart (7)

5 Exhausted (5,3)

9 Hoax call (5,5)

10 Tied the knot again (9)

11 Multi-talented sportsman (10)

13 Bind (in cloth) (7)

14 Piece of surgery (9)

20 Extermination of a race (8)

21 Petition (7)

22 Animate (7)

23 Fish stew (7)

*See answer 212*

# JIG-WORD

No clues – just pattern and answers – but can you fit them in?

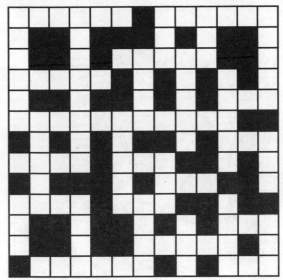

| 3-letter words | 4-letter words | SLOPE |
|---|---|---|
| AIM | BATH | TENSE |
| ASS | ECHO | TROUT |
| BAN | ISLE | |
| DAB | MEET | **6-letter words** |
| GAS | NODE | FURORE |
| HIT | TOUR | INSTEP |
| INN | | INSURE |
| MAN | | WITHIN |
| MET | **5-letter words** | |
| OLD | AISLE | **8-letter word** |
| PAY | DEALT | UNDULATE |
| TAG | FORTH | |
| THE | NAKED | **11-letter word** |
| WON | RADII | PARATROOPER |

See answer 212

# KRISS KROSS

In the top picture, the antique dealer is selecting a vase. In the bottom picture he has made his choice. Which vase did he choose?

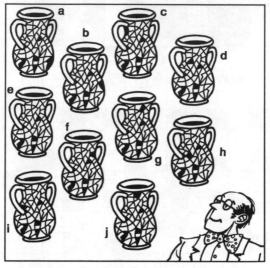

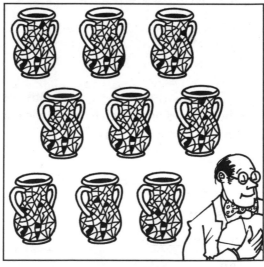

*See answer 212*

# PURPLE PASSAGE

In a Purple Passage, the grid of letters consists of an entertaining short story, reading across the rows from left to right and from top to bottom. However, some letters have been missed out. Not only that, but there are no spaces between words and no punctuation. Can you fill in the missing letters and work out where the word-breaks are to reveal the story?

| A | ☐ | A | T | W | A | S | L | ☐ | I | N | G | I | N | A | ☐ | A | T | C |
| ☐ | O | F | ☐ | U | N | L | I | G | H | ☐ | A | N | ☐ | G | E | T | T | I | N |
| ☐ | V | E | ☐ | Y | H | ☐ | T | ☐ | H | Y | D | O | N | T | ☐ | O | U |
| ☐ | O | V | E | O | U | T | O | ☐ | T | H | E | ☐ | U | N | ☐ | F | Y | O |
| ☐ | R | E | T | O | ☐ | H | O | ☐ | A | S | K | E | D | H | I | ☐ | F |
| ☐ | I | E | N | D | W | ☐ | Y | S | H | ☐ | U | L | D | I | R | E | ☐ | L | I | E | D |
| ☐ | H | E | C | A | ☐ | I | ☐ | A | S | ☐ | E | R | E | F | ☐ | R | S | T |

# SO COMPLETE

ARTHUR, MICKEY, LESLEY, FREDA, BERT, GREG, MEG, MILDRED, BUNTY, and TIM were remembering their favourite nursery-rhyme characters. Use the letters of their names once each to reveal the names.

```
TH_  G__ND  O__  D_K_  OF  _O__

HU_P__  DU_P__

O__  K___  _OL_

L__T__  _I_S  M__F__

OL_  _OT_E_  HU____D

G_O__I_  PO____
```

See answer 213

# TWO-TIMER

Two sets of clues to the same answers. Cryptic clues below and straight clues beneath the grid.

### ACROSS

6 Paddy, before morning, about ten, his natural disposition (11)

8 Bend weapon (3)

9 Monthly return of tropical food (3)

10 Admires intricate weapon (7)

12 Perfume despatched as announced (5)

13 Make light of getting to the point (5)

14 Tiny Scotch (3)

16 Handy way to demonstrate a pet affection (6)

17 Inspiration from Bertha (6)

18 Move up and down, to and fro (3)

20 Higher cut? (5)

22 What kangaroo has gently expressing pain (5)

23 Strike section of fortification (7)

24 Reptile amongst the cobras perhaps (3)

26 Turned up with band-leader at inn (3)

27 Stuffy preservationist? (11)

### DOWN

1 Tree second person mentioned (3)

2 It's separate, this decision (5)

3 Architectural feature to leave you cold, it is reported (6)

4 Clever sergeant-major had skill (5)

5 Unspecified number stuck in the canyon (3)

6 Come into contact with one working in the pool? (5-6)

7 One on the lookout for gifts (6,5)

10 One might need a rest during this game (7)

11 Companion very much supporting seaman (7)

14 Flycatcher on the internet (3)

15 Some pebbles might be exposed by it (3)

19 Bird that circles over its victim (6)

21 Fanatical bard I disconcerted (5)

22 Get ready to fire first (5)

25 Apt sort of tap! (3)

26 Greek character Penny is in reflective mood (3)

## ACROSS

**6** Moodiness (11)

**8** Front of a ship (3)

**9** US sweet potato (3)

**10** Handgun (7)

**12** Odour (5)

**13** Waxed spill (5)

**14** Very small (3)

**16** Sweep of an oar (6)

**17** Inhalation (6)

**18** Short haircut (3)

**20** Superior (5)

**22** Pocket (5)

**23** Defensive mound (7)

**24** Venomous snake (3)

**26** Tavern (3)

**27** One who stuffs animals (11)

## DOWN

**1** Churchyard plant (3)

**2** Diverge (5)

**3** Decorative band (6)

**4** Quick-witted (5)

**5** Whichever (3)

**6** Office worker (5-6)

**7** Entertainments recruiter (6,5)

**10** Indoor game (7)

**11** Sailor (7)

**14** Tangle (3)

**15** Recede (3)

**19** Fish-eating hawk (6)

**21** Zealous (5)

**22** Chief (5)

**25** Gentle 16 Across (3)

**26** 23rd Greek letter (3)

*See answer 213*

# MINESWEEPER

This puzzle has no clues in the conventional sense. Instead, every different number printed in the main grid represents a different letter (with the same number always representing the same letter, of course). For example, if 7 turns out to be a 'V', you can write in V wherever a square contains 7. We have completed a very small part of the puzzle to give you a start, but the rest is up to you.

| 25 | 15 | 1 | 3 | 7 | 22 | 5 | | 17 | 12 | 1 | 8 | 8 |
|----|----|----|----|----|----|----|----|----|----|----|----|----|
| 2 | | 21 | | 22 | | 9 | | 12 | | 3 | | 12 |
| 4 | 21 | 8 | 20 | 8 | | 8 (S) | 12 | 21 | 4 | 20 | 15 | 6 |
| 19 | | 1 | | 1 | | 12 (H) | | 20 | | 9 | | |
| 21 | 18 | 8 | 2 | 4 | 18 | 1 (E) | 11 | | 8 | 22 | 21 | 20 |
| 13 | | | 13 | | 11 | | 23 | | 5 | | 15 |
| 7 | 19 | 21 | 5 | 1 | 8 | | 18 | 9 | 4 | 1 | 21 | 9 |
| 26 | | 11 | | 11 | | 8 | | 26 | | | 22 |
| 1 | 22 | 26 | 6 | | 8 | 16 | 9 | 1 | 1 | 14 | 1 | 11 |
| | 21 | | 23 | | 9 | | 22 | | 2 | | 1 |
| 18 | 21 | 22 | 11 | 21 | 22 | 21 | | 7 | 22 | 22 | 1 | 4 |
| 7 | | 17 | | 17 | | 10 | | 15 | | 1 | | 1 |
| 18 | 15 | 1 | 21 | 24 | | 24 | 22 | 1 | 21 | 11 | 1 | 11 |

A B C D E F G H I J K L M
N O P Q R S T U V W X Y Z

(The small grid is provided for ease of reference only)

| 1 | 2 | 3 | 4 | 5 | 6 | 7 | 8 | 9 | 10 | 11 | 12 | 13 |
|----|----|----|----|----|----|----|----|----|----|----|----|----|
| 14 | 15 | 16 | 17 | 18 | 19 | 20 | 21 | 22 | 23 | 24 | 25 | 26 |

*See answer 213*

# ARROWORD

The arrows show the direction in which the answer to each clue should be placed.

| Major city on the Caspian Sea ▼ | Weak Long Island politician ▼ | ▼ | Loosened | ▼ | Big rooms | ▼ |
| ▶ | Spanish ranch | Form a surface for walking on | 1970 hit for the Kinks ▼ | Fringes ▼ | | |
| ▶ | Came up with | __ Gay, famous US bomber ▼ | Likelihood ▶ | | | Magical or mystical Hindu text |
| Wrong live broadcast ▶ | | | | Flurry ▼ | | ▼ |
| ▶ | | Aid illegally ▶ | | | | |
| Capri-corn __, 1978 film | | Darts players' line ▼ | Crikey, it's hot! ▼ | Uncle Sam's initials? (inits) ▶ | | |
| Runs with easy strides | | | | | __ Lingus, Irish plane company ▼ | |
| ▶ | | | Shabby articles ▶ | | | |
| 18th-century German composer | Former Austrian coin ▶ | | | | | |
| Person of Hebrew origin | | | Generation ▶ | | | |

See answer 213

# CRYPTIC CROSSWORD

### ACROSS

1 Spectacular holiday wear? (4,7)
7 Wicked deliveryman? (5,6)
8 Endlessly tense ballet-step (3)
10 Service address (6)
12 Responded when Swede ran amok (8)
13 Speak falsely with fellow in confidence (6)
14 A weapon in catalogue for scaremonger (8)
17 Penny, this cheap storybook, how terrible (8)
18 From mixed maintop, remove name having most favourable points (6)
19 Replaced at recent interval (8)
21 In spring, Dan skied in Poland (6)
23 Fashion of the century (3)
24 Unsympathetic and tough in the middle? (4-7)
26 Ubiquitous honour in returning gift (11)

### DOWN

1 Mother, almost noble lady (3)
2 Hurry to get things planted and become exhausted (3,2,4)
3 Shine but scowl unhesitantly (4)
4 Everything together that's fashionable taken in by a pair of learners twice (3,2,3)
5 Animal shut up about beginning of winter (5)
6 Foreman's oversight? (11)
7 Being insubordinate, ordered inside to bed (11)
9 Distracted, having been removed from mainline (11)
11 Becoming slower when dealing with notes (11)
15 Reject idea put re reconstruction (9)
16 Flatter now fat's increased (6,2)
20 Anglo-Saxon layer of wood (5)
22 Last home for woman with many children (4)
25 Bird entitled to appear within (3)

*See answer 213*

# WRAPPING UP

Have double the fun with this puzzle: you've got to fill in the answers and the black squares! We've given you the bare bones to start and it will help you to know that the black squares in the finished grid form a symmetrical pattern, so that every black square has at least one other corresponding black square.

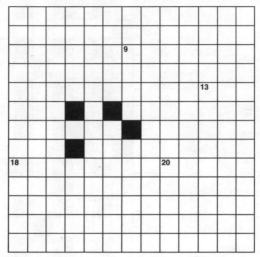

## ACROSS

1 Murmur
5 Mendacious
8 Short poem evoking rustic life
9 Self-mortification
10 Obesity
12 Up to the time of
14 Sagging
16 Frill
18 Low-ranking office worker
19 Wide pasta strips
22 Skewered
24 Top
26 Old silver coin
27 Day of rest

## DOWN

1 Unpleasant smell
2 Frosty
3 Regular beat
4 Lie back
5 Slow, relaxed
6 Coaching house
7 Species of goose
11 Treasure ___, valuable find
13 Object, item
14 Adorning, dressing
15 Small flat crumpet
17 Dashing fellows!
20 Firework
21 Drive (a fox) to its underground lair
23 Non-amateur
25 Small round vegetable

*See answer 213*

# CROSSWORD

## ACROSS

5 Sporty (8)

7 Tell porkies! (3)

8 Award for valour (5)

9 Caper (8)

11 Important test (4)

12 Con (4)

14 Soap bars (5)

15 Park yourself (3)

16 Female inheritor (7)

20 Go ___, become rotten (3)

21 Underlying foundation (5)

23 Claptrap, twaddle (4)

24 Drifting ice (4)

26 Active support (of a cause) (8)

28 Vex (5)

29 Once round a track (3)

30 Candidate (8)

## DOWN

1 Topples (5)

2 Style of knot (10)

3 Edible flesh from cattle and sheep (3,4)

4 Incorrect identification of a disease (12)

6 Lessen (9)

10 Thaw out (2-3)

13 Impute (7)

17 Display of great gratitude or approval (12)

18 ___ work, deep-level dental procedure (4-5)

19 Burnt remains (5)

22 Part of a cruet set (4,6)

25 Synthetic fibre (7)

27 Sudden outbreak (5)

*See answer 213*

# BACKWARDS

For this puzzle, we've filled in the answers, but there are letters in the grid, where the black squares should be. You need to black out the unwanted letters to make a symmetrical grid to match the clues, which are listed in random order.

| C | H | I | R | O | P | O | D | I | S | T |
|---|---|---|---|---|---|---|---|---|---|---|
| O | E | N | A | D | A | R | U | T | T | E |
| N | R | S | N | I | G | G | E | R | E | L |
| T | O | O | W | N | E | E | G | O | W | E |
| E | L | F | E | N | T | M | U | M | A | P |
| N | O | T | E | R | O | E | S | A | S | H |
| T | I | E | L | F | E | W | A | N | T | O |
| M | R | S | E | A | S | H | I | C | A | N |
| E | H | T | A | D | P | O | L | E | V | I |
| N | O | R | M | O | U | S | A | M | O | S |
| T | E | M | P | E | R | A | M | E | N | T |

**ACROSS**

- Young frog
- Be in debt (to)
- Musical symbol
- Maiden name indicator
- Foot health expert
- Pixie
- Remains of a fire
- Pale
- Half-suppressed laugh
- Woman's title
- Female relation
- As well
- Disposition
- Is able to
- Low marshy land
- Sliding window

**DOWN**

- Fashion, trend
- Beat
- Happiness
- Jewel
- World power
- Boy servant
- Unit of electrical current
- Novel about love
- Country hotel
- Moved swiftly
- Switchboard operator
- Urge on
- Most yielding
- Expected
- Which person
- Snake-like fish

See answer 214

# JOLLY MIXTURES

In this puzzle, each clue is simply an anagram of the answer – but watch out! There might be more than one possible solution to each clue. For instance, the clue 'TALE' might lead to the answer 'LATE' or 'TEAL'. You'll have to look at how the answers fit into the grid to find out which alternative is correct.

**ACROSS**

| 1 | PIERCE | 19 | REGAL |
| 4 | RIVING | 21 | ODE |
| 9 | ART | 24 | BEAD |
| 10 | SCION | 25 | NEAT |
| 11 | ITS | 28 | PIT |
| 12 | EARN | 30 | NAMED |
| 14 | GORE | 31 | DOH |
| 16 | ARE | 32 | SUNDER |
| 18 | ZONED | 33 | CRONES |

**DOWN**

| 1 | NEUTER | 16 | DEN |
| 2 | ARC | 17 | LEA |
| 3 | SHOP | 20 | RATTAN |
| 5 | CHIN | 22 | ENDOW |
| 6 | SAG | 23 | REEFED |
| 7 | TENTED | 26 | CAME |
| 8 | RUNIC | 27 | LIED |
| 13 | OATEN | 29 | RAP |
| 15 | ANGLE | 31 | ASH |

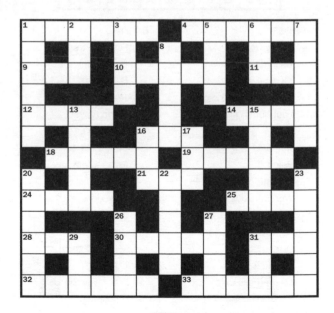

*See answer 214*

# CROSSWORD

When the letters of the answers from the upper grid are transferred to the lower grid, they give a quotation. Reading down column 'A' will give the name of its author.

| | |
|---|---|
| 1 | Perimeter fence |
| 2 | Following; warmth |
| 3 | Sabre; reckless |
| 4 | Make up; auction item |
| 5 | Slack; pledge |
| 6 | Paradise; foot digit |
| 7 | Beneath; tender |
| 8 | Unite; display |
| 9 | Proof |

Upper grid columns: A B C D E F G H J K (rows 1–9)

Lower grid:

| 3B | 8B | | 1D | 5E | 6K | 3E | | 2J | 9F | 5B | 6H | 8H | 4D | 7E |
| | | | | | | | | | | | | | | , |
| 1B | 2E | | 8J | 7K | 5K | 9E | 1G | 3J | | 2C | 5C | | | |
| | | | | | | , | | | | | | | | |
| 7G | 5H | 4F | 9C | 3A | 2B | 1H | | 2K | 6A | 9H | | | | |
| 9G | 3D | 2A | 6D | 4A | 7B | 8D | 5D | | 3C | 7J | | 6J | 7A | 8C |
| 3K | 1C | 8A | 6C | 4B | | 2G | 9A | 1F | 3G | 4K | 8G | | 8K | 2D |
| | | | | | | | | | | | . | | | |
| 6F | 7D | 2H | 9D | | 5J | 7H | | 4H | 5G | 4C | 8E | | | |
| 3H | 4E | 1E | | 1A | 6B | | 5A | 4J | 9B | 6E | 7C | | | |
| | | | | | | | | | | | . | | | |

*See answer 214*

# ROUND TOUR

A fantastic puzzle in which each square counts at least twice – some count three or four times! The answer-words form two continuous chains, each of them starting at the top left-hand corner and following the directions of the arrows to and fro along alternate rows, and down and up along alternate columns. Moreover, the last letter of one word is the first letter of the next one. For example, the three consecutive words GINGER, RED and DAVID would appear in the completed puzzle as GINGEREDAVID, so be careful – it's not an easy puzzle!

## TO AND FRO

- Original letter (7)
- Jemmy left Eve right (5)
- Reel around British revolutionary (5)
- Cover learner and one deputy head (3)
- Maiden changed me, lads! (6)
- Spikes shoestrings (5)
- Give voice to South African youth leader (3)
- Thread account (4)
- Love east Egyptian flower (4)
- Mires muddy Arabian rulers (5)
- See round in French river (5)
- One new vast age (3)
- Mesh after tax (3)
- Underground small pipes (5)
- Alarms temptresses (6)
- Small elf ego (4)
- Little lie about thread (5)
- A teen messily consumed (5)
- Northern primate scruff of neck (4)
- Reg oddly gets new yen for vitality (6)
- Closely unite obscure returned toy (3)
- Lukewarm new soft diet (5)
- Doctor, for example wine sediment (4)
- Silence joke (3)
- Leg back to take shape (3)
- Jumps over strange lapse (5)
- Dispatched perfume, we hear (4)
- Drink the health of brown bread (5)
- Stepped in retro device (4)
- Overshadow midget (5)
- Feathery leafed plant right in fen (4)
- On after no midday (4)
- No British toff (3)
- Scottish feature where there was a vicar, we hear (4)
- Big Australian bird you hear behind 'em (3)
- New World article after us (1,1,1)
- Al gets left every one (3)
- Hawaiian garland that is left around (3)
- Saint follows in present month (4)
- Pasta, possibly Spanish snacks (5)
- Sport new leather razor sharpener (5)
- Tack in softly before (3)
- No point at the moment (3)
- We are endlessly dressed in (4)
- Corruption to right coming back (3)

## DOWN AND UP

- Beg Eric to stir frozen mass (7)
- Chat about American petrol (3)
- Season old sailor (4)
- Russian author from lost toy (7)
- Affirmative you old son! (3)
- Girl is a sun's creation (5)
- Love duck (3)

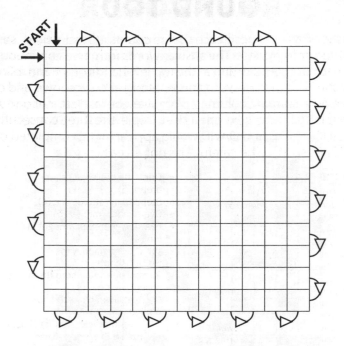

- The French can for language (5)
- No time for negation (3)
- Rue after time constant (4)
- Pause before a time period (3)
- Point gun at first class male (3)
- US city changed re my note (8)
- Yes it disturbed legendary Himalayan beasts (5)
- Sean becomes rational (4)
- Points around gym sword (4)
- Need new paradise garden (4)
- Topical material sewn round (4)
- Cuts old sayings (4)
- Snap new bridge arch (4)
- Norma got left as usual (6)
- Roads in Milan especially (5)
- Cut off bargain (4)
- Separate component (4)
- A hundred not returned (3)
- Seize new head sailor (3)
- Small nail British Rail advert (4)
- Comedian Jack or river (3)
- Dine out Miss Blyton (4)
- Bad end with evil Satan (5)
- Cheerful song till adapted! (4)
- Time referee is not kosher (4)
- Penny of backward dandy (3)
- Just beat hard seed (3)
- New plane console (5)
- Odd elf on a sheet of paper (4)
- One who touches antenna (6)
- About a thousand sun radiation units (4)
- Blockade inside Aussie gear (5)
- Sore about Greek god (4)
- Classify type (4)
- Chinese guild gripping device endlessly (4)
- Grab assorted clothes (4)
- Bung British rib east (5)

See answer 214

# KEYWORD

This puzzle has no clues in the conventional sense. Instead, every different number printed in the main grid represents a different letter (with the same number always representing the same letter, of course). For example, if 7 turns out to be a 'V', you can write in V wherever a square contains 7. We have completed a very small part of the puzzle to give you a start, but the rest is up to you.

| 18 | 17 | 5 | 13 | 15 | 12 | 20 | | 8 | 14 | 21 | 12 | 3 |
|----|----|----|----|----|----|----|----|----|----|----|----|----|
| 11 | | 26 | | 17 | | 12 | | 12 | | 14 | | 22 |
| 6 | 3 | 14 | 8 | 9 | | 5 | 26 | 14 | 15 | 17 | 5 | 12 |
| 15 | | 17 | | 2 | | 14 | | 13 | | 3 | | |
| 17 | 9 | 9 | 11 | 12 | 9 | 20 | 19 | | 25 | 12 | 14 | 7 |
| 25 | | | | 3 | | 12 | | 5 | | 25 | | 14 |
| 26 | 22 | 6 | 3 | 17 | 20 | | 24 | 19 | 3 | 4 | 12 | 23 |
| 12 | | 3 | | 12 | | 5 | | 9 | | | | 17 |
| 3 | 19 | 11 | 4 | | 7 | 14 | 3 | 16 | 19 | 3 R | 14 A | 7 M |
| | | 25 | | 16 | | 7 | | 11 | | 14 | | 17 |
| 12 | 25 | 1 | 11 | 17 | 3 | 12 | | 2 | 14 | 10 | 12 | 25 |
| 8 | | 11 | | 15 | | 3 | | 14 | | 19 | | 12 |
| 12 | 24 | 12 | 9 | 4 | | 14 | 15 | 15 | 11 | 3 | 12 | 20 |

**A  B  C  D  E  F  G  H  I  J  K  L  M**
**N  O  P  Q  R  S  T  U  V  W  X  Y  Z**

(The small grid is provided for ease of reference only)

| 1 | 2 | 3 | 4 | 5 | 6 | 7 | 8 | 9 | 10 | 11 | 12 | 13 |
|----|----|----|----|----|----|----|----|----|----|----|----|----|
| 14 | 15 | 16 | 17 | 18 | 19 | 20 | 21 | 22 | 23 | 24 | 25 | 26 |

*See answer 214*

# CROSSWORD

## ACROSS

**1** False head of hair (3)

**8** Maze-like (12)

**9** Drink taken with milk or lemon (3)

**11** Selected randomly (5)

**12** Absorb (7)

**14** Challenge to do something risky (4)

**15** Cigarette container (6)

**18** Metalworker (6)

**20** Corrosive liquid substance (4)

**23** Release your grip (5,2)

**25** Make one (5)

**27** Number of seats on a tandem (3)

**28** Soft (drink) (3-9)

**29** Make ___ while the sun shines, proverb (3)

## DOWN

**1** Aquatic ball game played by swimmers (5,4)

**2** Happy (4)

**3** Wear away by friction (6)

**4** Crush (5)

**5** Facial expression of scorn or contempt (5)

**6** Ruffian, hoodlum (4)

**7** Countless (6)

**10** Space science (9)

**13** In mint condition (3)

**16** Colouring pencil (6)

**17** Label showing a product's price (3)

**19** Fit to be eaten (6)

**21** ___ potato, person who watches a lot of television (5)

**22** Territory of a nobleman (5)

**24** GCSE, eg (4)

**26** Engrave (4)

*See answer 214*

# MISSING LINKS

The answer to each clue is a word which has a link with each of the three words listed. This word may come at the end (eg Head linked with Beach, Big and Hammer), at the beginning (eg Black linked with Beauty, Board and Jack) or a mixture of the two (eg Stone linked with Hail, Lime and Wall).

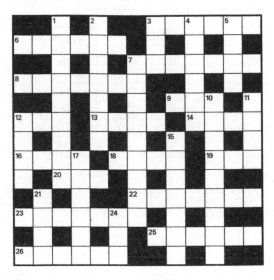

**ACROSS**

3 Bare, Needle, Worm (6)
6 Career, Rope, Step (6)
7 Branch, Constable, Offer (7)
8 In, Lounge, Van (7)
9 Band, Chair, Pit (3)
12 Form, Gallery, Nouveau (3)
13 Addict, Dealer, Store (4)
14 Birth, Blind, Dinner (4)
16 Noon, School, Sky (4)
18 Board, Gazer, Shooting (4)
19 Bath, Guard, Skipper (3)
20 Cauliflower, Mark, Ring (3)
22 Intervals, Triangle, Verb (7)
23 Fish, Sea, Wood (7)
25 Scout, Ship, Union (6)
26 Lamp, Level, Measure (6)

**DOWN**

1 Point, Take, Unfair (9)
2 Cabinet, Manner, Table (7)
3 Hat, Notch, Secret (3)
4 Breaker, Company, Hit (6)
5 Far, Game, Run (4)
7 Bone, Molecular, Social (9)
10 Breakfast, Orange, Tree (9)
11 Bird, Poppy, Vessel (4)
12 Head, Heart, Tooth (4)
15 Finger, Happy, Off (7)
17 Home, Sledge, Yellow (6)
21 Cold, Dragon, Shot (4)
24 Cracker, Hazel, Roast (3)

*See answer 214*

# CHEERS!

Have double the fun with this puzzle: you've got to fill in the answers and the black squares! We've given you the bare bones to start and it will help you to know that the black squares in the finished grid form a symmetrical pattern, so that every black square has at least one other corresponding black square.

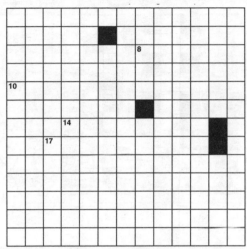

**ACROSS**

1 Originally a long open vehicle
5 Afternoon meal
7 Move around an axis
8 Troops' assigned quarters
9 ___ volatile, smelling salts
10 Euro-Asian mountain range
12 W Indian song, often improvised
13 Larva of a louse adhering to human hair
14 Old Russian autocracy
18 Add (up)
20 Just arrived (baby)
23 Main heart artery
24 Jailbird
25 Obstruct
26 Famous Florence art gallery
27 Wander about
28 One who delivers to homes

**DOWN**

1 Avoiding
2 Robert ___, director of M*A*S*H
3 Performers
4 Slight fever
5 Spring flowers
6 Official go-ahead
8 Bleat of a sheep
9 Terrifying
11 Ignited
15 Managed (by)
16 Make a noise like a cow
17 Took without permission
19 Axiom
21 1997 George Michael hit
22 John ___, 19th-century Arctic explorer

*See answer 215*

# FOURSOME

This man would like to buy four identical ornaments. Which design will he choose?

# SILHOUETTE

Shade in every fragment containing a dot – and what have you got?

*See answer 215*

# KEYWORD

This puzzle has no clues in the conventional sense. Instead, every different number printed in the main grid represents a different letter (with the same number always representing the same letter, of course). For example, if 7 turns out to be a 'V', you can write in V wherever a square contains 7. We have completed a very small part of the puzzle to give you a start, but the rest is up to you.

| 10 | 1 | 16 | 5 | 8 | 15 | | 26 | | 5 | 24 | 19 | 4 |
|----|----|----|----|----|----|----|----|----|----|----|----|----|
| 16 | | 20 | | 7 | 4 | 21 | 6 | 10 | 15 | | 4 | |
| 12 | 24 | 4 | 20 | 5 | 25 | | 22 | | 4 | 10 | 14 | 10 |
| 24 | | | 4 | | 11 | | 3 | 16 | 18 | 5 | | 4 |
| 16 | 22 | 7 | 14 | 16 | | 16 | | 18 | | 20 | | 1 |
| 22 | | 20 | | 9 | 24 | 13 | 5 | 4 | 14 | 7 | 10 | 16 |
| | | 6 | | 16 | | 14 | | 8 | | 1 | | |
| 16 | 21 | 21 | 6 | 8 | 6 | 16 | 18 | 5 | | 16 | | 25 |
| 3 | | 6 | | 5 | | 22 | | 10 | 16 | 3 | 2 | 16 |
| 2 | | 8 | 4 | 10 | 5 | | 19 | | 4 | | | 4 |
| 16 | 23 | 16 | 18 | | 20 | | 4 | 16 | 20 | 6 I | 4 | 22 |
| | 7 | | 5 | 20 | 24 | 10 | 5 | 11 | | 8 C | | 7 |
| 5 | 17 | 16 | 16 | | 16 | | 10 | 16 | 22 | 16 E | 8 | 5 |

**A B C D E F G H I J K L M**
**N O P Q R S T U V W X Y Z**

(The small grid is provided for ease of reference only)

| 1 | 2 | 3 | 4 | 5 | 6 | 7 | 8 | 9 | 10 | 11 | 12 | 13 |
|----|----|----|----|----|----|----|----|----|----|----|----|----|
| 14 | 15 | 16 | 17 | 18 | 19 | 20 | 21 | 22 | 23 | 24 | 25 | 26 |

*See answer 215*

# DATELINE

A number jig with a difference: with clues to figure out (with the help of a calculator if you wish!) to discover the date in the shaded line – in this case, a notable day in sporting history.

## ACROSS

**1** Add 3 Across to 5 Across

**3** Subtract 1,745 from 12 Down

**5** Divide 10 Down by 12,000

**7** Square root of 6,724

**8** Subtract 33 Across from 9 Across

**9** Digits of 3 Across reversed

**11** Add 130 to 1 Across

**13** Spots on eight dice

**14** Multiply 26 Down by eight

**16** Subtract 136,017 from 20 Down

**21** Add 84,196 to one-third of 16 Across

**22** Add 3,520 to the square of 5 Across

**25** Add 311 to 8 Across

**27** Multiply 7 Across by four

**28** Sum of all whole numbers from one to fifteen

**30** 24 baker's dozens

**31** Add four to years in a diamond wedding

**32** Add 500 to 29 Down

**33** Roman CIII

**34** Digits of 5 Across reversed

## DOWN

**1** Multiply 33 Across by 27

**2** Multiply 26 Down by the square root of 34 Across

**4** Feet in 74 yards

**5** Multiply 3 Across by nine

**6** Pounds in 343 stones

**9** Square of 1 Down

**10** Seconds in twenty days

**12** Digits of 1 Down reversed

**15** Subtract bingo's 'legs' from 1 Down

**17** 25 per cent of 10,100

**18** Add 1 Across to 5 Across, then subtract three

**19** Subtract 8 Across from 26 Down

**20** Multiply 2 Down by four

**23** Multiply 29 Down by twenty, then subtract 1,561

**24** Add 1 Down to one-tenth of 29 Down

**26** Add 6 Down to 23 Down

**29** Subtract 27 Across from 8 Across

*See answer 215*

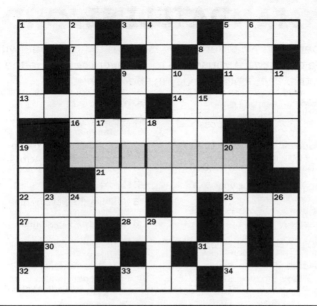

# SYMBOLIC

Can you work out which symbol should logically appear in the empty box, and which way up it should be?

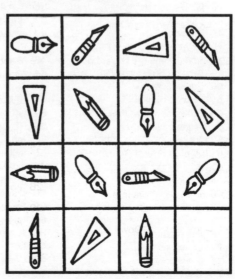

See answer 215

# GIANT CROSSWORD

## Across

1 Change in appearance (9)
5 Scenery at rear of stage (8)
9 Head of corn (3)
10 Colourless gas (5)
11 Funeral director (8)
12 Shoulder blade (7)
14 Game played on a course (4)
16 Collector of discarded material (8)
18 Worker who belongs to a trades group (8)
20 Pelt or hide (4)
22 Outlet of river to sea (7)
23 Poppycock! (8)
26 Archaeological relic (6)
29 Lost (7)
32 Hen's produce (3)
33 Tutoring (8)
34 Law officer (7)
35 Enchant (7)
37 Vow (4)
38 Nine-sided polygon (7)
42 Fall to a lower level (7)
45 Retained (4)
46 Relating to pottery (7)
48 Conforming (7)
49 Extremely pleasing (8)
50 Epoch (3)
51 Wishful thinker (7)
55 Brownish-yellow (6)
57 Angering (8)
59 Tussle (7)
61 Stretches (out) (4)
63 Commemoration (8)
64 Relocate (8)
66 Seat (4)
67 Written communication (7)
71 Preset explosive device (4,4)
72 Full amount (5)
73 Conclusion (3)
74 Sieve (8)
75 Refrained (9)

## Down

1 Narrow depressions (7)
2 Looks (4)
3 Vegetable (lady's fingers) (4)
4 Bill of fare (4)
5 Bosom (6)
6 Rectangular road stones (7)
7 Ms Smith, of culinary fame (5)
8 Depiction (9)
13 Dry red Italian table wine (7)
15 Smokestack of a ship (6)
17 Drinking vessel (5)
19 Call for help (1,1,1)
21 Bird of New Zealand (4)
24 Badly behaved (7)
25 Devon city (6)
26 Delicate, fragile (5)
27 Educational establishments (7)
28 Set alight (7)
29 Stonecutter (5)
30 Rear of ship (5)
31 Resistance against attack (7)
36 Run away (7)
39 Herb used in cooking (7)
40 Cause to be amazed (7)
41 Ruler (7)
43 Mode of expression (5)
44 Avid (5)
46 Circus entertainer (5)
47 Deliverance (6)
52 Lifting (7)
53 Heavenly beings (6)
54 Relieve (4)
55 Inflammation of the stomach (9)
56 Awkward, stupid people (5)
58 Maiden name indicator (3)
60 Disappointment (7)
62 Fastened with a metal pin (7)
63 Person in a group (6)
65 Purgative (5)
68 Mixer drink (4)
69 Unfortunately (4)
70 Sicilian volcano (4)

*See answer 216*

# STORY CROSSWORD

Transfer the words which complete the story to the grid and then put the circled letters in the right order to discover the name of the famous person therein described.

The ___ (12A) of a farmer, he is thought to have been born in about 1635, in Llanrhymny in Wales. He grew up in the ___ (22A) of the English civil war in a Royalist area, and he was still a young ___ (20A) when he made up his mind to join the army. His parents would not allow ___ (23D) to go but but he left anyway, ___ (31A) away to Bristol where he hoped to catch a stagecoach to London.

___ (6A) his hopes of winning glory on the battlefield were dashed though, when he was kidnapped by slave ___ (17D) in Bristol and taken across the ___ (15A) to Barbados, where he was sold to a ___ (5D) master.

For the next seven ___ (7D) years he worked on a sugar cane plantation, a brutal existence that gave him plenty of time to ___ (28A) the day he had left home.

Eventually, at the ___ (9A) of about nineteen, he ___ (8A) from his ___ (33A). He could have returned to Wales, but ___ (26A) old life seemed such a long time ___ (29D) that he chose to stay in the West Indies and join a pirate ___ (25D).

By 1666, he was in command of his own ship and became a feared but ___ (18D) figure. Held in great ___ (14D) by women and highly respected by his own ___ (10A), he was the scourge of the Spanish, attacking their ships and towns in ___ (4D) of savage piracy.

He would never attack British vessels though and ___ (32A) always willing to ___ (27D) to the assistance of the British navy when their ships came under attack from the Spanish. After driving the Spanish away from the British fleet near Cuba, he was made ___ (6D) of the Jamaican navy.

Shortly afterwards, Britain and Spain signed a peace treaty and Charles II ordered him to stop attacking the Spanish. He ___ (11D) already made plans to attack ___ (13A) though – a country reputed to contain fabulous wealth.

Ignoring the king's command, he ___ (3D) off for South America, determined to ___ (21D) his goal to ___ (16A) more gold to his treasure store.

He sacked Panama, but on his return to Jamaica he was arrested for piracy and taken to prison in ___ (2D) to face a possible ___ (18A) sentence. In his cell, he wrote numerous letters to Charles II entreating him to consider his ___ (24A).

For two ___ (1A) he had no reply, then the Spanish launched an attack on the British fleet and the war between Britain and Spain broke out again.

He was ___ (30A) out of prison and knighted for his loyalty. Charles II awarded him a ___ (19D) job, making him governor of Jamaica.

He died in 1688.

*See answer 216*

# KNOT SO

Can you work out how many of the tangles will form a knot when their ends are pulled?

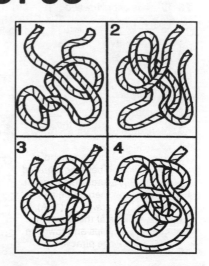

See answer 216

# CROSSWORD

## ACROSS

1 Female aristocrat (8)

6 17th-century soldier with a firearm (9)

7 Collection of items for auction (3)

8 Foolishly sentimental (5)

9 Wind instrument (8)

12 Naked and unclothed (4)

13 Reflection of sound waves (4)

16 Alternative therapist (9)

18 Course plotter (9)

19 Plan (4)

20 Units of electrical resistance (4)

23 Having a rough texture (8)

26 Refill (3-2)

27 Voice disapproval (3)

28 Expanse of brushwood (9)

29 Give rise to (8)

## DOWN

1 Pleasing (6)

2 Restless (9)

3 Store of valuable things (8)

4 Make higher (7)

5 Hunter's victim (4)

10 Bristled stick for mouth care (10)

11 Inconsiderate (10)

14 Shoreline (5)

15 Large branch (5)

17 Cinema film (5)

21 Bed's endpiece (9)

22 Guilty (8)

24 Common painkiller (7)

25 Owner (6)

26 Elephant's long tooth (4)

*See answer 216*

# JIG-WORD

Two sets of clues to the same answers. Cryptic clues below and straight clues beneath the grid.

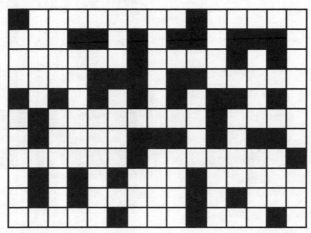

**3-letter words**
ASH
FAT
FIT
FLO
MAO
MOA
NUT
SHY
TOR
YES

GOAT
LAME
LOAF
LORE
OGEE
PIER
POOR
RELY
TALC
TOLL

**6-letter words**
ALLURE
ARMPIT
CACTUS
CELLAR
EXTORT
PETROL
TRADER

**7-letter words**
APOLOGY
RIPPLED

**4-letter words**
ALTO
BLOB
BYRE
ECHO

**5-letter words**
CORGI
CREEP
ERATO
OBOES
SHEAR
TOWER

**8-letter words**
ARTISTIC
CLEANSER

*See answer 216*

# TWO-TIMER

Two sets of clues to the same answers. Cryptic clues below and straight clues beneath the grid.

### ACROSS

**1** Absolutely delighted in space (4,3,4)

**9** Run off to fasten the door (4)

**10** Not an upright desire? (11)

**11** Departed, but not right (4)

**14** Lie about bran (5)

**17** Means to move house (5)

**18** Pole composed motet (5)

**19** Five, giving shout of pain, testify (5)

**20** She might tend to make others feel better (5)

**21** Each number had been taken in (5)

**22** It turns back and forth (5)

**25** Some advertisements featuring drink (4)

**29** Sticky fruit? (6-5)

**30** Upsetting Leon at Christmas time (4)

**31** It's topping for the hunter (11)

### DOWN

**2** Violet takes nearly new vegetation (4)

**3** Usual thing for a government to do (4)

**4** Some North Indian language (5)

**5** Tom takes up alternative form of transport (5)

**6** Money some took to Bologna (4)

**7** Person of little importance had ninety-ton monstrosity (9)

**8** Formal account from New Testament (9)

**12** Ten madmen corrected alteration (9)

**13** Asked to enter date wrongly (9)

**14** Alternatively leaving forever having infectious disease (5)

**15** Frank is not keen (5)

**16** Theatrical number (5)

**23** Make a tender suggestion? (5)

**24** Open using ball on the green (5)

**26** One is not at work to receive this pay (4)

**27** Old friend's gem (4)

**28** True colour? (4)

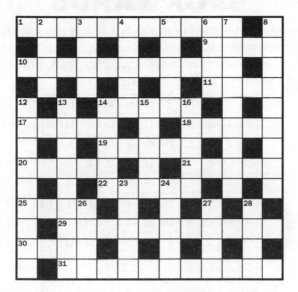

## ACROSS

**1** Elated (4,3,4)
**9** Dash, escape (4)
**10** Tendency (11)
**11** Abandoned (4)
**14** Thread (5)
**17** Minister's home (5)
**18** Carved pole (5)
**19** Bear witness (5)
**20** Medical assistant (5)
**21** Consumed (5)
**22** Revolving aerofoil (5)
**25** Wine made with honey (4)
**29** Caramel-coated fruit on a stick (6-5)
**30** Yuletide (4)
**31** Peaked hat (11)

## DOWN

**2** Grape plant (4)
**3** Reign (4)
**4** Indo-European language (5)
**5** Car (5)
**6** Ancient Greek coin (4)
**7** Insignificant person (9)
**8** Declaration (9)
**12** Improvement (9)
**13** Beseeched (9)
**14** Extreme state of excitement (5)
**15** Plain-spoken (5)
**16** Upper air (5)
**23** Bid (5)
**24** Public (5)
**26** Unemployment pay (4)
**27** Milky stone (4)
**28** Sad (4)

*See answer 216*

# BACKWARDS

For this puzzle, we've filled in the answers, but there are letters in the grid, where the black squares should be. You need to black out the unwanted letters to make a symmetrical grid to match the clues, which are listed in random order.

| S | T | A | R | T | U | S | A | B | R | E |
|---|---|---|---|---|---|---|---|---|---|---|
| A | I | S | U | I | C | I | D | E | O | N |
| U | P | P | E | R | O | T | O | A | S | T |
| C | U | E | B | E | R | E | T | S | E | E |
| E | R | N | E | T | H | O | S | T | A | R |
| A | S | H | W | H | I | T | E | A | S | T |
| P | U | C | E | R | N | E | T | H | I | N |
| O | I | L | R | F | O | B | C | O | D | E |
| S | T | A | L | E | R | R | U | L | E | R |
| E | A | S | I | A | M | E | S | E | N | V |
| R | I | S | E | R | O | W | A | S | T | E |

**ACROSS**
- Lubricate
- Before
- Billiards stick
- From Thailand
- Begin
- Diocese
- Rancid
- Part of a shoe
- Poem set to music
- Squander
- Celebrity
- Sea eagle
- Monarch
- Drink one's health
- Not fat
- Sword
- Part of a stair
- Watch chain
- Self-destruction
- Pure colour
- Purplish-red

**DOWN**
- Fatigue
- America's initials
- The coast
- Female sheep
- Make beer
- Creature
- Regret
- Untruth
- Building land
- School form
- Commotion
- Trembling poplar
- Coagulate
- Teaser
- Go in
- Horned African creature
- Gaps
- Ketchup, for example
- Dread
- Daring
- Chase

*See answer 217*

# JOLLY MIXTURES

In this puzzle, each clue is simply an anagram of the answer – but watch out! There might be more than one possible solution to each clue. For instance, the clue 'TALE' might lead to the answer 'LATE' or 'TEAL'. You'll have to look at how the answers fit into the grid to find out which alternative is correct.

## ACROSS

7 PEDANT
8 NEARER
9 DEN
10 MOAT
11 TOED
12 ART
14 DEALT
17 BAGEL
19 CODER
20 THESE
22 HATED
24 DAD
26 RITE
28 MODE
29 GNU
30 SACHET
31 GLIDER

## DOWN

1 TABLET
2 MITE
3 TAPED
4 RACED
5 RAID
6 LINTEL
13 NAMED
15 EEL
16 CAT
17 DOG
18 BAR
21 EIGHTH
23 PELMET
24 GLEAN
25 DOING
27 SORE
28 READ

*See answer 217*

# DATELINE

A number jig with a difference: with clues to figure out (with the help of a calculator if you wish!) to discover the date in the shaded line – in this case, the birthdate of a comedian.

## ACROSS

**1** Twice 5 Across

**5** Square root of 26 Down

**7** Multiply 25 Across by 249, then add 96

**8** Add 39,317 to 11 Down

**9** Square 30 Across

**11** Square root of 49,284

**13** First three digits of 5 Down

**15** Square 2 Down

**20** Multiply 2 Down by 5 Down

**21** Divide 9 Across by 4

**23** Multiply 1 Across by 5 Across

**25** Half of 4 Down

**27** Multiply 5 Across by 1,000

**28** Multiply 25 Across by 501, then subtract 10,000

**30** Divide 31 Across by 3

**31** Square root of 4,356

## DOWN

**1** Half of 31 Across

**2** Multiply 30 Across by 25 Down

**3** Twice 11 Across

**4** Multiply 31 Across by 4

**5** Half of 2 Down

**6** Add 2 to 31 Across

**10** Add 3,534,539 to 15 Across

**11** Square 151

**12** Add 24,000 to 21 Across

**13** Multiply the first two digits of 26 Down by 593

**14** Multiply 13 Across by 102

**16** Last three digits of 7 Across

**17** Subtract 618 from 16 Down

**18** Add 74 to 11 Across

**19** Multiply 30 Across by 37

**22** Multiply 21 Across by 30 Across

**24** Multiply 5 Across by 21 Across

**25** Next in series 59, 73, 87, ...

**26** Multiply 1 Across by 8

**27** Divide 7 Across by 2,747

**29** Add 4 to 30 Across

See answer 217

# PATHFINDER

Starting from the bold centre letter, move up or down or sideways (but NOT diagonally) to find the path through eighteen nautical terms.

| O | R | L | L | Y | A | R | E | I | T | T |
|---|---|---|---|---|---|---|---|---|---|---|
| W | C | A | A | B | W | W | L | L | E | L |
| S | T | S | A | N | G | A | O | W | B | E |
| N | R | I | G | R | E | T | T | L | I | F |
| E | A | N | A | M | E | C | R | N | U | E |
| S | M | K | R | A | **D** | K | E | D | I | D |
| T | E | N | N | U | F | B | Y | A | T | P |
| H | L | F | R | O | R | U | O | G | R | I |
| E | G | I | E | H | C | N | A | E | L | I |
| L | H | N | S | N | G | L | E | A | I | A |
| M | T | E | I | G | A | L | Y | M | N | S |

# CRYPTIC CROSSWORD

## ACROSS

**1** It is outdated as a painkiller for lumbago, perhaps (4-6)

**8** Another girl from Aileen (6)

**9** Song won't upset slum district (6,4)

**10** Separate act he'd developed (6)

**11** Like the youngest daughter, perhaps, at the back of the queue (4,2,4)

**12** Keep the soldiers in check (6)

**13** Head on one's shoulders (4)

**15** One who stirs up public interest endlessly is excited when dealing with notes (7)

**19** First male worker is intransigent (7)

**21** We split on a Welshman (4)

**22** Whistling when it's very hot (6)

**25** World-shattering experience (10)

**27** Obliquely across like the French book (6)

**28** I'd hum at first if I took the queen a moistener (10)

**29** String of invective from one in business (6)

**30** Vote to submit the last part to Greek character returning (10)

## DOWN

**1** Herb finds many in Iowa church (8)

**2** Youth leader following form that is elegant (6)

**3** Coypu had fruit before getting the wind up (6)

**4** Silver encountered Capone (5)

**5** Having done the plastering, submitted an account (8)

**6** Handyman – fellow to perform outside with hesitation (8)

**7** Idleness indeed (8)

**13** Keep under – lower! (3)

**14** Severely criticise the cooking vessel (3)

**16** Denied that profits help (8)

**17** One hurried to adjust the sails first of the boat (8)

**18** Three got tipsy at the same time (8)

**20** Met large eccentric with an urgent message (8)

**23** Landowner's singers, we hear (6)

**24** A diverse change without the last two – diverse (6)

**26** You're slim, egghead! (5)

*See answer 217*

# FOOD FUN

Arthur has cooked a cake, Bernard is wearing a scarf, Charles isn't wearing an apron, Daniel is wearing a low hat and Edward is standing next to Bernard. Can you put the names to the numbers?

*See answer 217*

# DOT-TO-DOT

Join the dots from 1 to 35 to reveal the hidden picture.

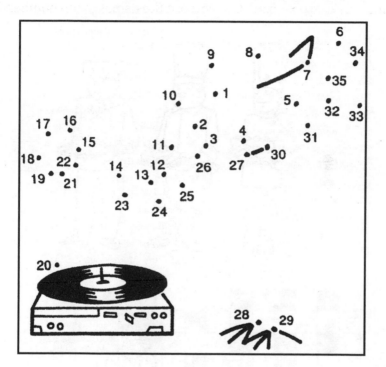

See answer 217

# CROSSWORD

**ACROSS**

4 Science of reasoned thinking (5)
9 Lithely (7)
10 For all to see (5)
11 Sprint, hurry (3)
12 Idiot (3)
13 Antagonist (3)
14 Hinted (7)
15 Professional varnishing (6,9)
19 Principal city (7)
20 Bed for a baby (3)
21 Mate (3)
22 In time past (3)
23 Children's entertainment (5)
24 Door attachment (7)
25 Sibling's daughter (5)

**DOWN**

1 Make redundant (3,3)
2 Musical rhythmic phrase (4)
3 Process of making into a god (11)
4 Medieval harp-like instrument (4)
5 Friendly (6)
6 Formation, construction (11)
7 Summertime star sign (6)
8 Breeding establishment (4)
16 Dilate (6)
17 Official residence of a sovereign (6)
18 Aplenty (6)
19 Manage (4)
20 Solid fuel (4)
21 Early infantry weapon (4)

*See answer 217*

# SAMPLER

A sample has been cut from each of the three rolls of cloth.
Can you tell which sample belongs to which roll?

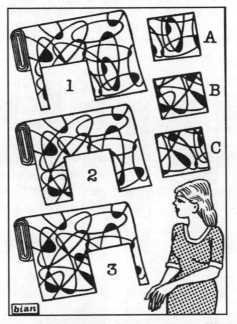

**150**

# 4-SQUARE

Solve these four clues and then rearrange the solutions into a
sixteen-letter phrase, for which a clue is given. The two diagonals
also make four-letter words.

CURVE, ARC

CHRISTMAS

MAKE AIRTIGHT

SMALL ARROW

Clue: He doesn't even come for the rent? (8,8)

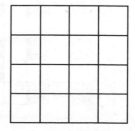

*See answer 217*

# KEYWORD

This puzzle has no clues in the conventional sense. Instead, every different number printed in the main grid represents a different letter (with the same number always representing the same letter, of course). For example, if 7 turns out to be a 'V', you can write in V wherever a square contains 7. We have completed a very small part of the puzzle to give you a start, but the rest is up to you.

| 20 | 5 | 17 | 1 | 24 | 10 | 13 | 10 | 13 |  | 23 | 8 | 10 |
|----|----|----|----|----|----|----|----|----|----|----|----|----|
| 2 |  | 25 |  | 13 |  | 10 |  | 17 |  | 5 |  | 24 |
| 21 | 15 | 12 | 24 | 17 |  | 17 | 18 | 2 | 3 | 15 | 24 | 9 |
| 15 |  | 12 |  | 11 |  | 20 |  | 5 |  | 1 |  | 10 |
| 17 A | 11 N | 24 T | 2 | 21 | 15 | 10 | 1 |  | 16 | 9 | 17 | 13 |
| 11 |  |  |  | 15 |  | 7 |  | 6 |  | 10 |  |  |
| 24 | 15 | 13 | 11 | 2 | 20 |  | 23 | 12 | 17 | 13 | 7 | 1 |
|  |  | 10 |  | 5 |  | 23 |  | 5 |  |  |  | 8 |
| 26 | 2 | 5 | 24 |  | 22 | 12 | 11 | 7 | 13 | 12 | 15 | 1 |
| 10 |  | 17 |  | 22 |  | 22 |  | 25 |  | 19 |  | 24 |
| 17 | 11 | 4 | 2 | 10 | 24 | 8 |  | 2 | 3 | 17 | 6 | 10 |
| 11 |  | 10 |  | 17 |  | 10 |  | 1 |  | 24 |  | 3 |
| 1 | 17 | 7 |  | 14 | 10 | 13 | 16 | 9 | 2 | 10 | 25 | 1 |

## A B C D E F G H I J K L M
## N O P Q R S T U V W X Y Z

(The small grid is provided for ease of reference only)

| 1 | 2 | 3 | 4 | 5 | 6 | 7 | 8 | 9 | 10 | 11 | 12 | 13 |
|----|----|----|----|----|----|----|----|----|----|----|----|----|
| 14 | 15 | 16 | 17 | 18 | 19 | 20 | 21 | 22 | 23 | 24 | 25 | 26 |

*See answer 218*

# ADD-A-LETTER

Insert or add a letter to these four-letter words to make five-letter
words which fit the rhyming clues. The six added letters should
spell out a word.

| | | |
|---|---|---|
| LUSH | | A velvety fabric of rich quality |
| SPAN | | Madrid's the capital of this country |
| QUID | | Tentacled creature of the ocean |
| HEAR | | Vital organ – keeps blood in motion |
| CAST | | Cliffs and beaches bordering the shore |
| OVER | | Romantic interest, paramour |

*See answer 218*

# BLACK OUT

Can you see which one of the six letters was printed by the reverse stamp which is shown at the top?

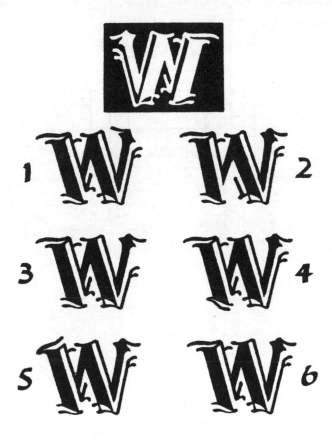

See answer 218

# SPIRAL

Every answer (except the first) uses the last letter of the preceding answer as its initial letter, the chain thus formed following a spiral path to the centre of the grid. The diagonals spell out the names of two colours.

**START**

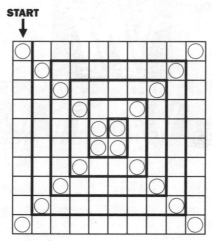

- Late December festival (9)
- Inactive, taking little exercise (9)
- Cede (5)
- Explanatory figure or plan (7)
- ___ Navratilova, Wimbledon champion (7)
- Covered with water (5)
- Occurrence, event (9)
- Deity (7)
- Take large steps (6)

- Of the highest excellence (9)
- Less difficult (6)
- Stiff, unbending (5)
- Twofold (6)
- Deceptive, shifty (7)
- Mistake (5)
- Monarch (5)
- Lion's noise (4)
- List of duties (4)
- Upper limb (3)

*See answer 218*

# BOXWISE

Put these three-letter groups into the twelve numbered boxes to produce twelve six-letter words, each of which starts in one box and finishes in another as indicated by an arrow. For instance, 2 and 5 make a six-letter word, but not 5 and 9. One group has been filled in to start you off.

HOR  TER  SET  PER

BAN  SON  NER  TEE

ROR  TAM  NET  ~~COR~~

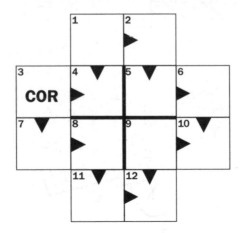

See answer 218

# IN THE ABSTRACT

George has bought one of the four abstract paintings shown here, but he can't remember which one it is or which way up it is supposed to go. Can you help him?

*See answer 218*

# STORY CROSSWORD

Transfer the words which complete the story to the grid and then put the circled letters in the right order to discover the name of the famous person therein described.

Although he was born in rural Kent, his early life was quite ___ (6D). He was first off to Ceylon where his father worked, then to America with his mother and sister, settling in San Francisco. Six months later, they moved on to Canada and eventually to New York. All this was before he was eight years old.

His mother decided he needed a proper education and brought him back to England, to Clifton College, Bristol. Here he had a ___ (12A) to show more ___ (7A) in sport rather than ___ (14A) work so, when the time came to leave, he had no idea what to do, but he decided on acting and enrolled with RADA. However, he would have to ___ (5D) before pursuing his theatrical life as, in 1940, his call-up papers arrived.

Desperate to see some action, he joined the Red Berets. There followed a ___ (23A) of ___ (13D) tests, until eventually he was declared unsuitable and was invalided out, much to his dismay.

___ (1D) on launching himself in films, he approached the director Carol Reed for a part, albeit a ___ (16D) one, in *The Way Ahead*. It was, however, the ___ (22A) his

___ (15D) needed. 1945 saw the release of *Brief Encounter*, which made him a ___ (11A), and he was to ___ (3D) this success in the equally ___ (24A) *The Third Man*.

When Jose Ferrer, the American actor-director, asked him to appear in the war picture *Cockleshell Heroes*, he could hardly ___ (9A), as he considered it to be the perfect opportunity to ___ (4D) international fame, and he was ___ (20A) right.

During the sixties and seventies, he was still ___ (21D) much in demand, although he wasn't always ___ (10A) in choosing film roles, as in the forgettable *Pope Joan*. But *Sons and Lovers* and ___ (18A) *Ryan's Daughter*, in which he was ___ (2D) to shed his military image and play a priest, are two of his finest.

The last years of his life were as busy as ever and, whereas many would have found the ___ (19D) too much, he kept working right up to his death, which came on January 7th, 1988, when he was ___ (8A) 71. His actress wife, Helen Cherry, was at his bedside. Together, they had remained a devoted ___ (17D) for more than forty years.

*See answer 218*

# VISIGRID

Can you see which one of these seven impressions was made by the stamp?

*See answer 218*

# TINKER, TAILOR

To discover who this person is unscramble the words in the verse, which hints at what the person does. Write these words into the boxes below, reading across, and, if you've placed them in the correct order, the arrowed column will spell out the occupation.

Visit this RATSIS'T LAPOURR if your whim

Is a colourful GINNAIPT on your KINS

CESETL a SINGED: an anchor, PHODLIN or bird,

And for sentimental PESTY, Mum's the DOWR.

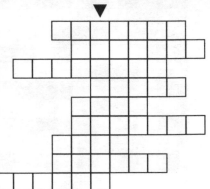

OCCUPATION: _____

# SILHOUETTE

Shade in every fragment containing a dot – and what have you got?

*See answer 218*

# NUMBER JIG

Just like a Jig-word – but instead of letters, numbers.

| 3-figures | 3745 | 5-figures | 79943 |
|-----------|------|-----------|-------|
| 331 | 3928 | 23333 | 84731 |
| 378 | 4788 | 28355 | 89033 |
| 511 | 5623 | 28814 | 93400 |
| 592 | 6442 | 35676 | |
| 732 | 7084 | 37389 | |
| 782 | 7113 | 38380 | |
| 791 | 7723 | 39005 | 6-figures |
| 905 | 7830 | 40298 | 371972 |
| | 8037 | 41173 | 378224 |
| 4-figures | 8129 | 42798 | 473211 |
| 1112 | 8387 | 61555 | 597826 |
| 2363 | 9327 | 68917 | 717775 |
| 3335 | 9893 | 77806 | 724520 |

*See answer 218*

# KEYWORD

This puzzle has no clues in the conventional sense. Instead, every different number printed in the main grid represents a different letter (with the same number always representing the same letter, of course). For example, if 7 turns out to be a 'V', you can write in V wherever a square contains 7. We have completed a very small part of the puzzle to give you a start, but the rest is up to you.

| 1 | 2 | 3 | 4 | 5 | 6 | 7 | 8 | 9 | | 10 | 11 | 12 |
|---|---|---|---|---|---|---|---|---|---|---|---|---|
| 11 | | 11 | | 11 | | 8 | | 2 | | 4 | | 2 |
| 3 | 11 | 13 | 2 | 14 | | 10 | 7 | 15 | 15 | 13 | 11 | 10 |
| 16 | | 7 | | 17 | | 17 | | 11 | | 18 | | 17 |
| 7 | 8 | 19 | 20 | 3 | 3 | 11 | 5 | | 16 | 7 | 17 | 11 |
| 8 | | | | 4 | | 1 | | 21 | | 8 | | |
| 9 | 6 | 1 | 10 | 20 | 22 | | 23 | 7 | 8 | 9 | 13 | 11 |
| | | 2 | | 10 | | 24 | | 11 | | | | 13 |
| 13 | 20 | 3 | 16 | | 13 | 2 L | 19 A | 3 C | 4 · | 10 | 10 | 11 |
| 20 | | 25 | | 26 | | 17 | | 19 | | 13 | | 19 |
| 8 | 4 | 20 | 3 | 7 | 10 | 26 | | 11 | 8 | 2 | 19 | 17 |
| 9 | | 11 | | 10 | | 11 | | 10 | | 10 | | 11 |
| 11 | 21 | 17 | | 10 | 19 | 3 | 2 | 17 | 19 | 26 | 11 | 5 |

## A B C D E F G H I J K L M
## N O P Q R S T U V W X Y Z

(The small grid is provided for ease of reference only)

| 1 | 2 | 3 | 4 | 5 | 6 | 7 | 8 | 9 | 10 | 11 | 12 | 13 |
|---|---|---|---|---|---|---|---|---|---|---|---|---|
| 14 | 15 | 16 | 17 | 18 | 19 | 20 | 21 | 22 | 23 | 24 | 25 | 26 |

*See answer 219*

# SYMBOLIC

Which two of the smaller rectangles contain the same four symbols?

# VISIGRID

Can you see which one of the seven prints was made by the roller?

See answer 219

# CROSSWORD

## ACROSS

4 Spider's snare (3)
8 Talk rapidly and incoherently (8)
9 Make clear (6)
10 Arise (4,2)
11 Steer (8)
13 Title of Russian emperors (4)
15 Alternative (5)
16 Rounded roof (4)
18 Name applied to a great Indian prince (8)
20 Underground exploring (6)
22 Direct (descendant) (6)
23 Make frail (8)
24 Conclusion (3)

## DOWN

1 Pinnacles (6)
2 Swallow greedily (4)
3 Prevent (4)
4 Misguided (5-6)
5 Large dam-building rodent (6)
6 ___ on, revolved around (6)
7 Hare's tail (4)
12 Female farm animal (3)
13 Male domestic cat (3)
14 Wanderer (6)
15 Word of a god (6)
17 Shawl (6)
19 Barren, parched (4)
20 Small restaurant (4)
21 Suddenly change direction (4)

*See answer 219*

# THAT BIT OF DIFFERENCE

There are eight differences between these two cartoons.
Can you spot them?

See answer 219

# TWO-TIMER

Two sets of clues to the same answers. Cryptic clues below and straight clues beneath the grid.

### ACROSS

**1** Pack member not meant to be taken seriously (5)

**4** Stage show featuring terrible act – going round undressed! (7)

**8** Barber's vessel (7)

**9** Fruit drink, about two pence (5)

**10** Bit of a scrap (5)

**11** Flower faeries dancing (7)

**13** One of some found in avenues or streets (4)

**15** Sweet, well-dressed person has the same point repeated (6)

**17** New Delhi's protection (6)

**20** A, B, C, D, F or G! (4)

**22** Fine goal (7)

**24** Bridget's heart is in the mountains (5)

**26** Man of parts (5)

**27** Eat nuts, strangely causing disease (7)

**28** Can rule out a type of energy (7)

**29** Encourage singularly good health (5)

### DOWN

**1** Kitty shot by sailor (7)

**2** If Ken moves, it will cut (5)

**3** Salesman allowed leading exporter to be well-stocked (7)

**4** Gunner in the restaurant has a bottle (6)

**5** How one might welcome you thus (5)

**6** Swift, sharp reply to tripe so awful (7)

**7** Character from Greece in the Territorial Army (5)

**12** Support the others (4)

**14** Split the hire charge (4)

**16** In fact, a crazy, over-enthusiastic type (7)

**18** Eric the Terrible doesn't follow the accepted doctrine (7)

**19** Welsh theatre attendant? (7)

**21** Peculiar story about Gravesend shellfish (6)

**22** It's obvious there's one in the plot (5)

**23** At which one has a lot of freedom (5)

**25** Square ball? (5)

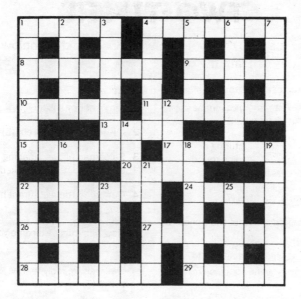

## ACROSS

- **1** Jester (5)
- **4** Night-club entertainment (7)
- **8** Sailing ship (7)
- **9** Green or red fruit (5)
- **10** Part (5)
- **11** Iris (7)
- **13** Woody plant (4)
- **15** Chewy sweet (6)
- **17** Plate of armour (6)
- **20** Message (4)
- **22** Forfeit (7)
- **24** Crest (5)
- **26** Performer (5)
- **27** Lockjaw (7)
- **28** Subatomic (7)
- **29** Applaud (5)

## DOWN

- **1** Top prize (7)
- **2** Piece of cutlery (5)
- **3** Completely filled (7)
- **4** Wine-flask (6)
- **5** Courageous (5)
- **6** Rejoinder (7)
- **7** Greek letter (5)
- **12** Relaxation (4)
- **14** Torn (4)
- **16** Zealot (7)
- **18** One with an unconventional belief (7)
- **19** Sideboard (7)
- **21** Bivalve (6)
- **22** Evident (5)
- **23** Great (5)
- **25** Move to music (5)

*See answer 219*

# CROSSWORD

## ACROSS

**1** Beastly (7)

**7** Picture stand (5)

**8** Place of underground excavation (3)

**9** After all others (4)

**10** Alcoholic drink (4)

**12** Be an onlooker (8)

**14** Clothing retailer (9)

**15** Minor planet (8)

**18** Gourd (8)

**21** Corporate label (9)

**23** Functioning (8)

**25** Long-billed wading bird (4)

**26** Steep rugged rock (4)

**28** Fiery (3)

**29** Muslim scriptures (5)

**30** Fatty (7)

## DOWN

**2** Stinging insects' home (5,4)

**3** Void (4)

**4** Having an irrational fear of the unknown (13)

**5** Isolated retreat (9)

**6** Affected (5)

**11** Make a great effort (6)

**13** Wear away (5)

**16** (In a position) on one's own say-so (4-9)

**17** High-pitched (5)

**19** Tired-looking (6)

**20** Aircraft propulsion device (3,6)

**22** Whale product used in perfume-making (9)

**24** Brief and profound (5)

**27** Deliberately omit (4)

*See answer 219*

# CROSSWORD

**ACROSS**

1 Evasive behaviour (13)

9 Unctuous (6)

10 Unseen danger for motorists (5,3)

11 Ankle-length skirt (4)

12 Number-calling game (5)

13 Person controlled by others (4)

14 Liquid mineral (3)

15 Bring charges against (3)

16 Small British garden bird (4)

18 Indicate or suggest without stating directly (5)

20 Slight mark (4)

22 Provide (a foreign film) with a written translation (8)

24 Blood fluid (6)

25 Deep thinking (13)

**DOWN**

2 Ballroom dance (5)

3 Particular way of telling a story (7)

4 Shaft of light (3)

5 Hut, cottage (5)

6 Cover for a brewing vessel (3,4)

7 Tree which grows from an acorn (3)

8 Flat-bottomed boat (4)

12 Burn mark (7)

13 Long narrow flag (7)

17 Profligate, rake (4)

19 Journalistic profession (5)

21 Brief film role (5)

23 Darken in the sun (3)

24 Baked pastry dish (3)

See answer 219

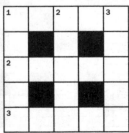

# TINKER, TAILOR ...

To discover who this person is unscramble the words in the verse, which hints at what the person does. Write these words into the boxes below, reading across, and, if you've placed them in the correct order, the arrowed column will spell out the occupation.

This person ASSUMERE you with a PEAT,

SUDJATS the UMDYM to your HASPE

And SKROW away with TAPLE and TRAD

To make a FAINOSH REMGNAT smart.

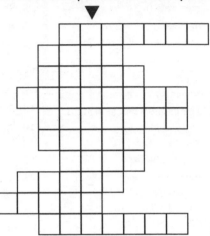

OCCUPATION: _____

# TAKE FIVE

The three answers in this mini-crossword read the same across and down. We've given you clues to the three words, but NOT in the right order. See how quickly you can solve it.

1 Beneath

2 Mistake

3 Small rodent

*See answer 219*

# JIG-WORD

No clues – just pattern and answers – but can you fit them in?

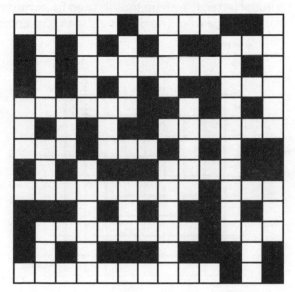

| 3-letter words | 4-letter words | PHRASE |
|---|---|---|
| AIL | AFAR | RECOIL |
| AND | FREE | WRECKS |
| BOX | ROTA | |
| EMU | SIDE | **8-letter words** |
| ERR | | ELEVATOR |
| NAP | **5-letter words** | SPITEFUL |
| NUN | APACE | |
| PAR | ARROW | **9-letter word** |
| PEA | COSTA | INTERVIEW |
| RAM | PINCH | |
| RED | | **10-letter words** |
| SET | **6-letter words** | BLANCMANGE |
| TAG | EXILES | QUADRUPLET |
| VIA | LEGEND | |

*See answer 220*

# LETTER SET

Every answer (except the first) uses the last letter of the preceding answer as its initial letter, the chain thus formed following a spiral path to the centre of the grid. The diagonals spell two English ports.

**START**

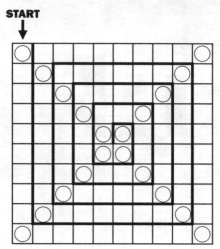

- Patron saint of animals (7)

- Rarely (6)

- Pilgrim Fathers' ship (9)

- Rice dish (7)

- Fertile desert spot (5)

- Extend (7)

- Soft felt hat (7)

- Male goose (6)

- Contrite (9)

- Bother (7)

- King Arthur's sword (9)

- Heating device (8)

- Round building (7)

- Similar (5)

- Join the army (6)

- Warty amphibian (4)

- Varied (7)

*See answer 220*

# BODY LANGUAGE

The Across clues consist of jumbled-up words relating to the body.
The Down clues and answers are normal.

**ACROSS**

3 FURSCF
6 ODNENT
7 LEADBDR
8 TAPEALL
9 ARE
12 MUG
13 PEAT
14 MILB
16 STUB
18 SIIR
19 TUG
20 OTE
22 SHEYLEA
23 SHUMREU
25 DIMELD
26 USITSE

**DOWN**

1 Person skilled in dissection (9)
2 Servings of ice-cream (7)
3 Roman sun god (3)
4 Type of tyre (6)
5 Jumping insect (4)
7 Electrical cells (9)
10 River forming border between the US and Mexico (3,6)
11 Assist in crime (4)
12 Hurtful remark (4)
15 One who lives austerely (7)
17 Tall structures (6)
21 Dame ___ Dench, Oscar-winning actress (4)
24 Function (3)

*See answer 220*

# GIANT CROSSWORD

## Across

1 Casino card game (9)
6 Down-payments (8)
10 Adam's Biblical partner (3)
11 Accurate (5)
12 Manufacturer (8)
13 Blood-red (7)
15 Metallic element (4)
17 Traditional practices (8)
19 Investigation (8)
21 Tells (4)
23 Took for granted (7)
24 Portable defence from rain (8)
27 More lustrous (8)
30 Members of a ship's crew (7)
33 Existed, lived (3)
34 Foot digit (3)
35 Illustrations, instances (8)
36 Land of fifty states (7)
37 Entertainment venue (7)
39 Consumes (4)
40 Transition (7)
44 External (7)
47 Ova (4)
48 Night attire (7)
50 Trying out (7)
51 Logs for burning (8)
52 Put into service (3)
53 Alcoholic beverage (3)
54 Attained (7)
58 Insistence (8)
60 Abandoned (8)
62 Relieve an itch (7)
63 Detritus (4)
65 Fabric (8)
66 Win approval or support for (8)
68 Reverberation (4)
70 Discharge (7)
74 Member of one's family (8)
75 Walk about stealthily (5)
76 Saucepan cover (3)
77 In a grave, sedate manner (8)
78 Twenty-four hours ago (9)

## Down

1 Gentle winds (7)
2 Once more (5)
3 Outfits (4)
4 Continent (4)
5 Main beam of a vessel (4)
6 Lowest regions (6)
7 Dither (13)
8 Difficult or unusual feat (5)
9 Give up (9)
14 Enclosed space (7)
16 Cursory (6)
18 Let in (5)
20 Unwell (3)
22 Domain (4)
25 Depressed (7)
26 Missing (6)
28 Occurs (7)
29 Chosen by vote (7)
30 Postal token (5)
31 Units, pieces (5)
32 Statuesque (7)
38 Adult male chicken (7)
41 More furious (7)
42 Female siblings (7)
43 Quantities (7)
45 Native to Eire (5)
46 Bordered (5)
48 Manner of uttering a word (13)
49 Adjudicated (6)
55 Competition submissions (7)
56 Embrace lovingly (6)
57 Greek love god (4)
58 Vital travel documents (9)
59 Mistake (5)
61 Epoch (3)
64 Basket on wheels (7)
65 Only just (6)
67 Cause fear in (5)
69 Combination of notes (5)
71 Noblewoman (4)
72 Requests (4)
73 Duelling sword (4)

See answer 220

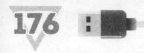

# KEYWORD

This puzzle has no clues in the conventional sense. Instead, every different number printed in the main grid represents a different letter (with the same number always representing the same letter, of course). For example, if 7 turns out to be a 'V', you can write in V wherever a square contains 7. We have completed a very small part of the puzzle to give you a start, but the rest is up to you.

| 23 | 5 | 8 | 13 | 15 | 13 | 25 | 23 | | 20 | 23 | 23 | 14 |
|----|---|---|----|----|----|----|----|---|----|----|----|----|
| 25 | | 22 | | 22 | | 12 | | 21 | | 9 | | 13 |
| 8 | 13 | 17 | 13 | 9 | | 6 | 18 | 12 | 16 | 16 F | 9 | 19 |
| 3 | | 7 | | 12 | | 6 | | 24 | | 4 I | | 10 |
| | 1 | 12 | 4 | 17 | 25 | 23 | 21 | 21 | 23 | 17 N | 8 | 23 |
| 13 | | 18 | | 25 | | 26 | | 23 | | | | 17 |
| 8 | 3 | 23 | 2 | 23 | 26 | | 21 | 1 | 12 | 4 | 18 | 25 |
| 18 | | | | 23 | | 18 | | 12 | | 17 | | 21 |
| 4 | 17 | 25 | 23 | 18 | 16 | 23 | 18 | 23 | 17 | 8 | 23 | |
| 10 | | 4 | | 4 | | 14 | | 17 | | 23 | | 10 |
| 22 | 18 | 6 | 13 | 17 | 11 | 13 | | 25 | 13 | 17 | 6 | 22 |
| 17 | | 23 | | 6 | | 4 | | 9 | | 21 | | 21 |
| 19 | 13 | 18 | 17 | | 6 | 18 | 23 | 19 | 17 | 23 | 21 | 21 |

A  B  C  D  E  F  G  H  I  J  K  L  M
N  O  P  Q  R  S  T  U  V  W  X  Y  Z

(The small grid is provided for ease of reference only)

| 1 | 2 | 3 | 4 | 5 | 6 | 7 | 8 | 9 | 10 | 11 | 12 | 13 |
|---|---|---|---|---|---|---|---|---|----|----|----|----|
| 14 | 15 | 16 | 17 | 18 | 19 | 20 | 21 | 22 | 23 | 24 | 25 | 26 |

See answer 220

# WORK FORCE

Can you see which three of these vases are exactly the same?

See answer 221

# ROUNDABOUT

Solutions to Radial clues (1 to 24) either start from the outer edge of the circle and read inwards, or start from the inner ring and read outwards to the edge (so they are all five-letter words). Solutions to Circular clues read in either a clockwise or an anticlockwise direction around the circle.

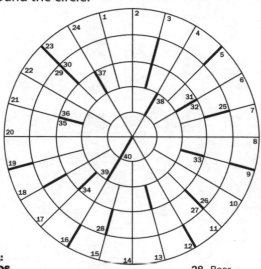

**RADIAL:**
**INWARDS**

2 Intended
3 Representative
5 King with a golden touch
6 Debtors
7 Russian emperors
8 ___ Enfield, comedian
9 Journal
10 Monastery
11 Full of punctures
12 Lock of hair
13 Pile up
15 Seasons
20 Unit of length
21 Lighthouse
24 Rainy snow

**OUTWARDS**

1 Abrupt, concise
4 Canonised person
14 Soak
16 Acer tree
17 Manufacturer
18 Skinflint
19 Florida city
22 Gives out
23 Ant

**CIRCULAR:**
**CLOCKWISE**

5 Night-flying insect
16 Go astray
19 Little demons
27 Great ___, feature of Llandudno

28 Beer
30 Otherwise
32 Organ of hearing
33 Competent
36 Objective
37 Period of time
38 Take into custody
39 Pilots

**ANTICLOCKWISE**

4 Most domesticated
11 Possessed, owned
15 Tiff
25 Flying appendage
26 Prejudice
29 Topic
31 Perish
34 Earnest prayer
35 Assignment
40 Modus operandi

*See answer 221*

# MISSING LINKS

The answer to each clue is a word which has a link with each of the three words listed. This word may come at the end (eg Head linked with Beach, Big and Hammer), at the beginning (eg Black linked with Beauty, Board and Jack) or a mixture of the two (eg Stone linked with Hail, Lime and Wall).

## ACROSS

3 Granny, Iron, Tyre (4)
6 Nymph, Pile, Pulp (4)
8 Acid, Check, Dance (4)
9 Earnings, Ink, Man (9)
10 Jumble, Price, Room (4)
11 Instructor, Jump, Lift (3)
12 Book, Comedy, Rough (6)
15 Hostile, Natural, Working (11)
19 Launcher, Science, Sky (6)
21 Afternoon, Break, Urn (3)
22 Bishop, Duke, Enemy (4)
23 Action, Picketing, School (9)
25 Garden, Reef, Slip (4)
26 Club, Express, Pit (4)
27 Calendar, Financial, Leap (4)

## DOWN

1 Elbow, Gun, Paint (6)
2 Bell, Mercy, Statement (7)
4 Assembly, Judge, Washing (4)
5 Cap, Quick, Time (8)
6 Penny, Stop, Wolf (7)
7 Crude, Filter, Olive (3)
9 Feeling, Fitting, Wind (3)
13 Flush, Spot, Water (3)
14 Fire, Persuasion, User (8)
15 Drum, Piercing, Trumpet (3)
16 Ceremony, Hollow, Roll (7)
17 Doing, Else, Much (7)
18 Belt, Net, Razor (6)
20 Small, Stir, Up (3)
22 Code, Office, Play (4)
24 Alter, Boost, Maniac (3)

See answer 221

# DILEMMA

Two straightforward crosswords – but their clues have been mixed up. You have to decide which clue belongs to which pattern, but two words have been entered to give you a start.

The crossword grid contains the letters **D O N O R** at position 18.

## ACROSS

| | |
|---|---|
| 1 Motive | 1 Smashed |
| 5 Mute | 5 Acquire |
| 9 School punishment | 9 Lebanese tree |
| 10 Spurn | 10 American space-station |
| 11 Natural fibre | 11 Cause to remember |
| 12 Uses sparingly | 12 Cricket team |
| 15 Many, lots | 15 Sheriff |
| 17 Sprint | 17 Barrel |
| 18 Giver | 18 Young man |
| 19 However | 19 Wager |
| 20 Droop | 20 US author |
| 22 Sifting implement | 22 Immunisation fluid |
| 24 Baby's bed | 24 Take a drink |
| 26 Found, discovered | 26 Isolated area |
| 27 Angel | 27 Tough coating |
| 28 Fix firmly | 28 Drums |
| 30 Guardian | 30 Ravel piece |
| 31 Speak | 31 Areas |
| 32 Main course | 32 Being |
| 33 Revolve | 33 Deprived |

## DOWN

| | |
|---|---|
| 1 Street musician | 1 Most scarce |
| 2 Life-giving gas | 2 Abut |
| 3 Inhabit | 3 Overjoyed |
| 4 Mesh | 4 Pen tip |
| 5 Dry, as wine | 5 Rowing blade |
| 6 Gap | 6 Line on a weather map |
| 7 Bury | 7 Bee colony |
| 8 Naturist | 8 Leaseholder |
| 13 Of the moon | 13 Prestige |
| 14 Famous | 14 Hard, dense |
| 15 Cooker | 15 Waterlily |
| 16 Uncanny | 16 Fable writer |
| 20 Sea-rover | 20 Constant, firm |
| 21 Red gemstone | 21 Bring out |
| 22 Nap | 22 Start a journey (3,3) |
| 23 Recollection | 23 Enclose |
| 24 Photographer's box | 24 Blot |
| 25 Celestial body | 25 Royal seat |
| 29 Pig-house | 29 Fish eggs |
| 30 Implore | 30 Spider's lair |

*See answer 221*

# PIECEWORD

With the help of the Across clues only, can you fit the 35 pieces into their correct positions in the empty grid (which, when completed, will exhibit a symmetrical pattern)?

## ACROSS

1 Meal; flatfish
2 Coax, cajole through flattery
3 Light rainstorm; spring festival
4 Charles _____, Victorian author
5 Coal spade; craving for liquid
6 Tall and thin
7 Fable; peak
8 Forerunner
9 Water vapour; trim feathers (of birds)
10 Flower's stem
11 Cooking instructions; young child
12 Female
13 Foundation; woodland clearing
14 Forged
15 Rural thoroughfare; brief letter
16 Command
17 Earthquake; morals
18 Heavy artillery, bombardment
19 Sorrow; maim
20 Unspecified person
21 More difficult; capital of Greece

188

CROSSWORD

**U R E** / **T** ⬛ **S** / **E N S**

**R E P** / **E** ⬛ **R** / **S H O**

**N S** ⬛ / **T H I** / **Y** ⬛

⬛ **M Y** / **A** ⬛ **P** / **S T E**

**R** ⬛ **A** / **I C S** / **B** ⬛ **S**

**I** ⬛ **T** / **S H O** / **T** ⬛ **T**

**I N J** / **N E** ⬛ / **A T H**

**T** ⬛ **E** / **T E R** / **E** ⬛ **I**

⬛ ⬛ **O** / **M O R** / ⬛ **B A**

⬛ **O** ⬛ / **A N T** / ⬛ **H**

⬛ **R** ⬛ / **E E D** / ⬛ **C** ⬛

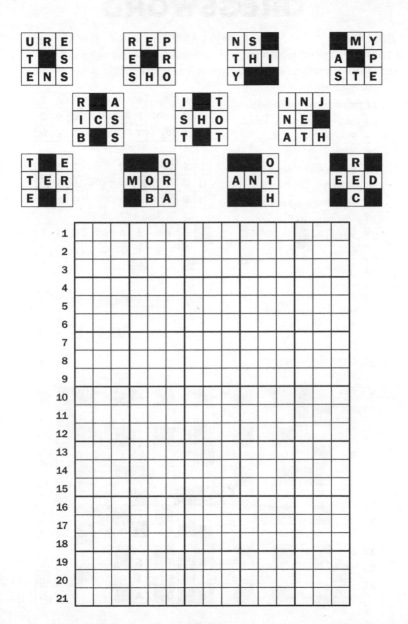

1
2
3
4
5
6
7
8
9
10
11
12
13
14
15
16
17
18
19
20
21

See answer 221

189

# CROSSWORD

## ACROSS

**1** Front part of overalls (3)

**8** Putting in the picture (12)

**9** Have regret for (3)

**11** Shrimp-like crustacean (5)

**12** Scramble to get on by fair means or foul (3,4)

**14** Lasting flavour (4)

**15** S American fruiting tree (6)

**18** Older relative, familiarly (6)

**20** Central church section (4)

**23** Be very sure (3,4)

**25** Prose piece (5)

**27** No longer in jail (3)

**28** Wastefulness (12)

**29** Rower's tool (3)

## DOWN

**1** Don't touch it with a ___, refuse to have anything to do with it! (9)

**2** Sound of a car horn (4)

**3** Delicate, of a fabric (6)

**4** Middleman (5)

**5** Unrelenting (5)

**6** Sea mile (4)

**7** Baby or young child (6)

**10** Future state (9)

**13** Turkish governor (3)

**16** Showing curiosity (6)

**17** Including (3)

**19** Overlooked (6)

**21** In agitation (5)

**22** Spookily odd (5)

**24** Skilful (4)

**26** Child's toy on a string (2-2)

*See answer 222*

# CROSSWORD

## ACROSS

**5** Unity, solidarity (8)

**7** Wet-weather garment (3)

**8** Staple Italian food (5)

**9** Cue (8)

**11** Exclude (4)

**12** Amend proofs (4)

**14** Study intensively within a short period (3,2)

**15** Miss the mark (3)

**16** Harmful (7)

**20** Curve section (3)

**21** Sub-machine gun (5)

**23** Plus (4)

**24** Former Indian coin (4)

**26** Imagine, picture (8)

**28** Weapon of chivalry (5)

**29** Alcoholic drink distilled from sugar cane (3)

**30** Ambitious person (8)

## DOWN

**1** Idle or mischievous person (5)

**2** Cooking additive (10)

**3** Sterile (7)

**4** Lack of balance (12)

**6** Inland Revenue form (3,6)

**10** Insect larvae (5)

**13** In large amounts (7)

**17** Unswerving quality (12)

**18** Trinket (9)

**19** Obscure or secluded path (5)

**22** Relating to administration (10)

**25** Hermit (7)

**27** Forge worker (5)

*See answer 222*

# JIG-WORD

No clues – just pattern and answers – but can you fit them in?

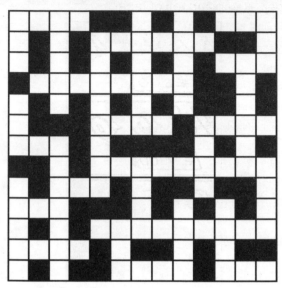

### 3-letter words
ACT
APE
ERR
ION
LEA
POT
SAY
SUN
TAG
TOY

### 4-letter words
BEST
EDIT

FREE
FRET
POST
ROTA
RUIN
RUSE
SATE
SOFT

### 5-letter words
DELTA
FLEAS
TIFFS

### 6-letter words
ADDING
LAMENT
TRADER

### 7-letter word
TRANCED

### 8-letter words
CASEMENT
TREASURE

### 9-letter words
DETERGENT
REPORTAGE

*See answer 222*

# SUM-UP

Using the totals given, can you calculate the price of each envelope, pen, stamp and roll of tape?

# 4-SQUARE

Solve these four clues and then rearrange the solutions into a sixteen-letter phrase, for which a clue is given. The two diagonals also make four-letter words.

THIN STRIP OF WOOD

BEARDED FARM ANIMAL

PIT

LADDER STEP

Clue: Serious affair (2,8,6)

See answer 222

# KEYWORD

This puzzle has no clues in the conventional sense. Instead, every different number printed in the main grid represents a different letter (with the same number always representing the same letter, of course). For example, if 7 turns out to be a 'V', you can write in V wherever a square contains 7. We have completed a very small part of the puzzle to give you a start, but the rest is up to you.

| 19 | 2 | 14 | 6 | 24 | 1 | | 26 | 16 | 24 | 13 | 6 | 1 |
|---|---|---|---|---|---|---|---|---|---|---|---|---|
| 18 | | 16 | | 18 | | 21 | | 4 | | 12 | | 18 |
| 4 | 24 | 2 | 6 | 26 | | 2 | | 6 | 10 | 23 | 18 | 12 |
| 12 | | 3 | | 19 | 18 | 1 | 19 | 20 | | 3 | | 23 |
| 6 | 21 | 14 | 6 | 1 | | 13 | | 1 | 2 | 14 | 7 | 19 |
| 19 | | | 12 | | 25 | 16 | 4 B | | 14 | | | 6 |
| | 5 | 6 | 4 | 24 | 18 | | 2 I | 3 | 12 | 18 | 20 | |
| 18 | | | 16 | | 8 | 23 | 14 G | | 16 | | | 9 |
| 26 | 12 | 16 | 22 | 3 | | 3 | | 1 | 16 | 4 | 6 | 24 |
| 26 | | 23 | | 6 | 17 | 2 | 1 | 19 | | 24 | | 2 |
| 18 | 3 | 14 | 6 | 24 | | 19 | | 24 | 16 | 16 | 8 | 1 |
| 2 | | 7 | | 15 | | 20 | | 18 | | 16 | | 16 |
| 24 | 18 | 19 | 7 | 6 | 24 | | 1 | 9 | 16 | 11 | 6 | 3 |

## A B C D E F G H I J K L M
## N O P Q R S T U V W X Y Z

(The small grid is provided for ease of reference only)

| 1 | 2 | 3 | 4 | 5 | 6 | 7 | 8 | 9 | 10 | 11 | 12 | 13 |
|---|---|---|---|---|---|---|---|---|---|---|---|---|
| 14 | 15 | 16 | 17 | 18 | 19 | 20 | 21 | 22 | 23 | 24 | 25 | 26 |

*See answer 222*

# CROSSWORD

**ACROSS**

1 Another term for the navy (6,7)

9 Flick through (pages) (6)

10 Happening (8)

11 Amaze (4)

12 Small flat savoury Indian cake (5)

13 Young animals (4)

14 Mongrel (3)

15 Only even prime number (3)

16 Eccentric (4)

18 Carved decoration (5)

20 Cylindrical hand warmer (4)

22 Remain firmly where you are (3,5)

24 Connect up to the electrical system (4,2)

25 Alternative (medicine) (13)

**DOWN**

2 Be (5)

3 First stage of human life (7)

4 Grass similar to wheat (3)

5 Girl's name or heather (5)

6 Mindlessness (7)

7 Much-eaten sea fish (3)

8 Small portion (of butter) (4)

12 Look after, rear (5,2)

13 Set fire to (7)

17 Dead keen (4)

19 Metric fluid measure (5)

21 Roving monk (5)

23 As well, besides (3)

24 Dish enclosed in pastry (3)

*See answer 222*

# STORY CROSSWORD

Transfer the words which complete the story to the grid and then put the circled letters in the right order to discover the name of the famous person therein described.

The son of a civil servant who made his name ___(27A) Arabia, he was born in Ambala, ___(8A) in 1911. He was educated at Westminster ___(1D), then went on to Trinity College, ___(7A), where he ___(16D) Guy Burgess, Donald Maclean and Anthony Blunt. They all shared an interest in communism and it soon became clear that the Soviet agents were keen to ___(3D) his name to their list of spies. He became an agent for them in 1933.

Following the outbreak of the Spanish civil ___(14A) in 1937, he went to Spain as a freelance journalist and a Soviet ___(25D). He was later employed by *The Times*.

In 1940 he returned to London and managed to ___(17D) a post with the British Secret Intelligence Service (MI6). This job gave him the opportunity to pass on secret information to his Soviet contacts. In 1944, he achieved the ___(15D) of head of the anti-communist counter-espionage unit. He used his position to prevent the defection to the west of ___(17A) of the KGB's senior officials, an occurrence which would have caused ___(11A) difficulties for the Soviet Union if it ___(5D) gone ahead. His part in the matter was ___(28A) detected and when World War II ended, he was awarded an ___(2D) for his wartime services.

In 1949 he ___(11D) off for the United ___(6D) to take up a post as the first secretary of the British embassy in Washington, where he worked closely with the CIA. Burgess ___(13A) posted to Washington by the Foreign Office, but before long he discovered that the security services were interested in Maclean's activities. He sent Burgess home to encourage Maclean to ___(26D) to get ___(24D) of Britain before it was too ___(12A). The ___(22A) men defected in 1951 and he was interrogated about his part in the affair. He denied all knowledge of any wrongdoing by either man. The investigators doubted that anyone ___(19A) was involved, but there was not ___(20D) evidence ___(21A) him to bring a successful prosecution. He was asked to resign from his post.

He worked as foreign correspondent for the *Observer* and the *Economist* in ___(4D), then took ___(9A) for the Soviet Union in 1963. He was granted political asylum and became a Soviet citizen. His wife ___(18D) to join him in Moscow, but she ___(10D) disenchanted with life there and returned to the West in 1965, leaving him ___(23A). In 1968 ___(5A) book, *My Silent War*, was published. He died in 1988.

# BOXWISE

Put these three-letter groups into the twelve numbered boxes to produce twelve six-letter words, each of which starts in one box and finishes in another as indicated by an arrow. For instance, 2 and 5 make a six-letter word, but not 5 and 9. One group has been filled in to start you off.

GER HAL HUN LED

LEN LET PAL SUL

TED TIL TRY VES

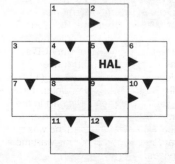

See answer 222

# SOLUTIONS

## PUZZLE 1

RADIAL: 1 Prial 2 Petty 3 Pesky 4 India
5 Inapt 6 Capri 7 Irish 8 Rache 9 Altar
10 Poser 11 Gazer 12 Aside 13 Aspen
14 Apart 15 Appal 16 Taste 17 Sweat
18 Treat 19 Smart 20 Haste 21 Arete
22 Eater 23 Eared 24 Prams
CIRCULAR: 5 Tay 6 Cheap 11 Gentlest
19 Shard 24 Sly 25 Tame 26 Kip
27 Ash 28 Load 29 Tare 30 Maw
31 Era 32 Ads 33 Picts 34 Zip 35 Apse
36 Ease 37 Trait 38 Earner 39 Sparta
40 Pirate

## PUZZLE 2

ACROSS: 1 Picnic 4 Pit 7 Auto
8 Protection 9 King 10 Soldier 14 Key
15 Sperm 17 Dry 18 Instant 23 Food
25 Engagement 26 Cane 27 Pet
28 Washer
DOWN: 1 Paper 2 Cross 3 Ideal 4 Prize
5 Tank 6 Standard 11 Dip 12 Rum
13 Personal 15 Ski 16 Rat 19 Night
20 Arena 21 Teeth 22 Water 24 Deep

## PUZZLE 3

```
R O U G H E N E D   D   P
  U   A   I   X   L E S S
P R O P A G A T E   F   E
S   E   H   R   M E N U
A   S   S T R A P   C   D
C L U M P   A   R E T R O
C   F   U M B R A   I   N
O F F E R   B   N A V V Y
M   U   S L I C K   E   M
P O S Y   O   A   I   B
A   I   A G I T A T I O N
N O O K   I   E   C   O
Y   N   S C O R C H I N G
```

## PUZZLE 4

```
  T   D O G E     O A R
V E R A     P L A N   A
  M   I N F E R   I   N
  P   S   A   E N F O L D
N O W   R   T   N   O
O   T O M   E   C   M
N O D   I N F A N T
A   R   K   C   N   A
G R E N A D I E R   C R Y
E   A   R   D   E A R N
  A R E A   I   D   E   S
  I   T W O   L A T E
I M A G E   M U M   K   T
```

## PUZZLE 5

ACROSS: 1 Strum 5 Strap 8 Egret
9 Iliad 10 Eager 11 Ankle 12 Shell
15 Latch 18 Grandchildren 19 Adore
22 Cress 25 April 26 Oscar 27 Alice
28 Leeds 29 Ferry 30 Petal
DOWN: 1 Swiss 2 Raise 3 Medal
4 Broken-hearted 5 Steel 6 Right
7 Parch 13 Herod 14 Liner 16 Alder
17 Chess 19 Aloof 20 Occur 21 Early
22 Clasp 23 Edict 24 Spell

ACROSS: 1 Cross 5 Cages 8 Choir
9 Miner 10 Abate 11 Aspic 12 Cheap
15 Kayak 18 Helter-skelter 19 Farce
22 Sweat 25 Monet 26 Diana 27 Angel
28 Inter 29 Sisal 30 Trend
DOWN: 1 Comic 2 Ounce 3 Scrap
4 Compassionate 5 Crack 6 Gravy
7 Sleek 13 Hyena 14 Attic 16 Allow
17 Arena 19 Fades 20 Reams
21 E-mail 22 Start 23 Eagle 24 Tiled

## PUZZLE 6

```
P   S C O F F   C A C H E   M
E V I L   L U N A R   E T N A
D   B O G U S   P E A C E   N
A X I S   T I T A N   T R O T
L   L E V E L   C A P O N   T
O V A T E   L   I   A R I S E
    N   T R A I T O R   T
M O T T O   D   O   T R Y S T
U   E   H E A R T   A   R
S C H E M E   B   A S T U T E
T O E   A D V A N C E   R I B
A W N I N G   T   K E N N E L
R   C   E L E G Y   E   E
D E T E R   I   R   F E T I D
    E   E M B R A C E   E
T E R S E   E   N   T H A N K
A   R U L E R   D R E A M   E
R A I L   R A T I O   I S L E
I   B L E A T   O V E R T   N
F I L E   S O U S E   D E A L
F   E N T E R   E R R O R   Y
```

## PUZZLE 7

Tin of peas – £1.00; bag of sweets
– £1.50; box of cornflakes – £1.75;
bottle of milk – £1.25

## PUZZLE 8

Tact, mare, hilt, mine. The phrase is:
MENTAL ARITHMETIC

## PUZZLE 9

| D | Y | N | A | S | T | | J | A | R | G | O | N |
|---|---|---|---|---|---|---|---|---|---|---|---|---|
| E | | I | | H | A | Z | E | L | | O | | U |
| F | A | C | T | O | R | | T | I | N | P | O | T |
| E | | E | | W | | G | | H | | M | | M |
| C | A | L | M | E | R | | T | H | I | E | V | E |
| T | R | Y | | D | E | P | O | T | | R | A | G |
| | S | | | | V | | Q | | | L | | |
| B | O | A | | N | E | X | U | S | | S | U | B |
| U | N | R | E | A | L | | E | A | S | I | E | R |
| L | | B | | T | | | M | | G | | | E |
| G | N | O | M | I | C | | S | P | O | N | G | E |
| E | | U | | V | O | W | E | L | | E | | Z |
| D | A | R | K | E | N | | G | E | N | T | L | Y |

## PUZZLE 10

ACROSS: 1 Abominable snowman
2 Donate; tail; tile; ore 3 Hospital; veal;
dense 4 Eternal; lecture; top 5 Rather;
oast; elevens 6 Expire; odd; ounce; can
7 Dean; answer; narrate 8 Camera;
erect; secret 9 Apply; seer; oil; allot
10 Spear; annoy; lotions 11 Person;
Derby; tingle 12 Inestimable; fog; rye
13 Add; gate; rioting; arm 14 Nicely;
natter; penal 15 Scan; enact; also; Eire
16 Eerie; Achilles; sten 17 Aster; peep;
bat; heart

DOWN: 1 Adhered; Caspian Sea 2 Boot;
axe; appendices 3 Onset; pampered;
cart 4 Map; Rhine; lass; genie
5 Itinerary; rota; leer 6 Net; arena;
sanity; nap 7 At a loose end; menace
8 Ballad; wren; earache 9 Lives; deer;
orbit; tip 10 Elector; coy; blot; alb
11 State; until; yet; Ella 12 Nil; ulna;
slot; fir; set 13 Old; recreation; Posh
14 Wee; ever; cling; geese 15 Monte
Carlo; granita 16 Arson; ate; only; rarer
17 Neeps; nett; seem; Lent

## PUZZLE 11

BEDTIME

## PUZZLE 12

ACROSS: 1 Bovine 5 Clammy 9 Ago
11 Seducer 12 Run into 13 Airy
15 Sheet 16 Walk 17 Lock 19 Brush
20 Opal 24 Sarcasm 25 Old hand
26 Own 27 Sensor 28 Eleven
DOWN: 2 Order 3 Inch 4 Earth tremor
5 Cornerstone 6 Aunt 7 Mania
8 Establish 10 Rockslide 14 Yak
16 Woo 18 Carve 21 Plate 22 Jags
23 Edge

## PUZZLE 13

The words in their correct order,
are: araBesque, dAncer, Leap, soLo,
entrEchat, piRouette, posItion,
audieNce, performAnce.
The occupation is: BALLERINA

## PUZZLE 14

## PUZZLE 15

ACROSS: 1 Communist 7 Marine
8 Earned 9 Rank 10 Seem 12 The
15 Died 16 Born 17 Set 18 Each
19 Done 21 Active 22 Return
23 Alienated
DOWN: 1 Committee 2 More
3 Unnerved 4 Speak 5 Concerns
6 Had 11 Mentioned 13 Educated
14 Foreseen 19 Dwell 20 Just 21 Any
The person described is:
JOSEPH McCARTHY

## PUZZLE 16

1 Wea 2 Pon 3 Sil 4 Ken 5 Cho 6 Sen
7 Ver 8 Bal 9 Gen 10 Try 11 Lad 12 Der

## PUZZLE 17

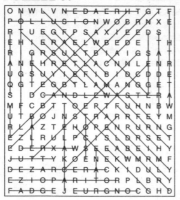

## PUZZLE 18

```
2 3 1 3 6   1   9   8 3 1 4 6
5   0   5     5 2 6 1 7   2   5
0   9   0   9   2   1   0     0
0   9   5 1 1     0   1   7   5
7 0 2 3 4     8 6 3   1 3 4 1 2
      9         9         9   0
7 0 9 1 3     1 7 1 0 2   1
4     3 4 2 6 1   0   6 2 5
5 1 3 0 8 4       3       4 0 7
  6       6 2 4 3 9 7   3
4 3 1 6 2   1 1 4   1 9 0 6 6
3     3   6 0 7   1         1
9 1 0 6 0   3   2   6 1 1 3 4
1     9 1 4   8 3 4         0
5 2 2 8 9   5 0 8   2 3 3 6 8
```

## PUZZLE 19

1 Rodent, drone, node 2 Impair, prima, prim 3 Cradle, clear, real 4 Stride, resit, rest 5 Stolen, stone, toes 6 Gyrate, grate, tear 7 Waddle, addle, lead 8 Caries, cares, cars 9 Mantle, metal, late 10 Choker, chore, Cher 11 Strung, grunt, trug.
The two games are: TIDDLYWINKS and RACING DEMON

## PUZZLE 20

Courteous – sickness – Seychelles
– sugar – redundant – Toronto
– orange – exercise – England
– Delilah – homework – kismet
– tavern – nuisance – emotional
– laburnum – manager – Rommel
– Lewis – snub – brew – William
– moth – hall – lard – dye
The two materials are:
CAVALRY TWILL and DOUBLE DAMASK

## PUZZLE 21

ACROSS: 1 Gumbo 4 Can 6 Washed out 7 Well-to-do 9 Margarita 10 Took 12 Help 14 Bewilder 17 Inactive 19 Inky 21 Glue 23 Inner city 25 Arsonist 27 Inventory 28 Nil 29 Where
DOWN: 1 Gown 2 Masseur 3 Overleaf 4 Crocodile 5 National park 8 Smuts 11 Opera 13 Firth 15 Devil 16 Civilisation 18 Beryl 20 King's evil 22 Brand new 24 In-store 26 Byte

## PUZZLE 22

| A | S | K | E | W |   |   |   |   |   | S |   | C |
| R |   |   | O | O | Z | E |   | S | E | E | R |
| R | U | G |   | R |   | N |   | N |   | N |   | U |
| E |   | O | G | L | E |   | L | I | F | T | E | D |
| S | R |   | R |   | D |   | A |   | I |   | E |
| T | A | I | L |   | D |   | R | E | A |
|   |   | L |   | L | A | R | G | E | N | E | S | S |
| A |   | L |   | R |   | E |   | D |   | H |
| S | H | A | T | T | E | R |   | V |   | E |
| P |   | H |   | A | G | O |   | V |   | I |
| E | A | G | E | R |   | G |   | T | H | A | W | S |
| C |   | E |   | H | E | R | E |   | D |   | L |
| T | A | L | O | N |   | D |   | M | E | T | E |

## PUZZLE 23

The girl bought apron g

## PUZZLE 24

ACROSS: 1 Blacksmith 6 Acid 9 Rub down 10 Inwards 12 Take advantage 14 Harlow 15 Asbestos 17 Mackerel 19 Soccer 22 Southern Ocean 24 Reserve 25 Sawbill 26 Warm 27 Prepayment
DOWN: 1 Barn 2 Arbiter 3 Knock together 4 Manual 5 Thievish 7 Currant 8 Dispensary 11 Winged one's way 13 Thumbscrew 16 Hear hear 18 Cruiser 20 Confine 21 Gossip 23 Blot

## PUZZLE 25

ACROSS: 1 Bestride 5 Scot 9 Daystar 10 Panel 11 Eft 12 Debris 15 Idiot 17 Oslo 19 Redden 22 Instal 24 Yawn 26 Cycle 27 Remark 30 Lea 32 Bambi 33 Parable 34 Toll 35 Splatter
DOWN: 1 Body 2 Style 3 Rotor 4 Duress 6 Consist 7 Tell-tale 8 Option 13 Bud 14 Iona 16 Brickbat 18 Line 20 Decimal 21 Eyelid 23 Spa 25 Wrap up 28 Maria 29 Rebut 31 Beer

## PUZZLE 26

Goalkeeper – Touchline – Crossbar – Referee – Centre circle – Sweeper – Ball – Goalpost – Substitute – Penalty spot – Striker – Goal line – Midfielder – Corner flag

## PUZZLE 27

## PUZZLE 28

ACROSS: 1 Practice 6 Misgovern 7 Old 8 Testy 9 Mountain 12 Oast 13 Scar 16 Salt marsh 18 Spectator 19 Inns 20 Acme 23 Narcotic 26 Bagel 27 Bit 28 Integrate 29 Rainy day
DOWN: 1 Pompom 2 Assiduous 3 Trotting 4 Chelsea 5 Only 10 Northerner 11 Possession 14 Carat 15 Amity 17 Lie in 21 Chipboard 22 Hooligan 24 Regatta 25 Steely 26 Bail

## PUZZLE 29

| S | O | B |   | S | I | N |   | P | I | G |
|---|---|---|---|---|---|---|---|---|---|---|
| E |   | I | M | P | R | O | V | E |   | U |
| E | B | B |   | A | I | D |   | W | A | N |
|   | R |   |   | D |   |   |   | B |   |   |
| P | A | L |   | L | E | A |   | A | S | P |
| A | D | O | L | E | S | C | E | N | C | E |
| N | A | G |   | I | C | E |   | D | O | T |
|   | W |   |   | E |   |   |   | N |   |   |
| O | L | D |   | A | N | T |   | A | D | D |
| R |   | R | A | U | C | O | U | S |   | A |
| B | A | Y |   | K | E | Y |   | K | I | D |

## PUZZLE 30

ACROSS: 1 Plea 5 Arch 8 Float 10 Shoot 11 Enrol 12 Rob 14 Ream 17 Able 19 Aligned 20 Star 21 Dame 22 Compile 23 Mash 25 Rent 28 Nor 30 Devil 32 Groin 33 Arson 34 Drop 35 Used
DOWN: 2 Loofa 3 Aft 4 Polo 5 Ate 6 Carob 7 Tsar 9 Flue 12 Railman 13 Bendier 15 Extra 16 March 17 Adder 18 Lemon 23 Mode 24 Sever 26 Erode 27 Tang 29 Oast 31 Lap 32 Gnu

## PUZZLE 31

1 Basement 2 Ahead, fret 3 Salary, sty
4 Infer, rife 5 Lethargic 6 Hound, rude
7 Upshot, bid 8 Minor, work 9 Envisage
Human love is rewarding for it brightens
up the day and makes the burdens of
life easier to carry.
Basil Hume

## PUZZLE 32

The unscrambled words in their correct
order are: Tall, gaRden, bEech, Elm,
chainSaw, cUt, expeRt, Grows, nEat,
Oak, braNches
The occupation is: TREE SURGEON

## PUZZLE 33

Mass, cape, fork, tare. The phrase
is: AS A MARK OF RESPECT

## PUZZLE 34

TO AND FRO: Pressing, glowers, shares,
skipper, ream, mittens, scares, score,
emir, remit, tea, appal, lean, newt,
tress, sale, erst, towed, dacha, algae,
end, deep, pain, nicer, rent, tail, Lisa,
about, terns, slept, triads, Sao, our,
root, toy, yes, sec, caller, Romeo
DOWN AND UP: Permit, tor, read, does,
sinews, steep, prepare, erect, tram,
moot, Tai, idea, aim, miss, skimp, plan,
nip, purer, relic, cap, pets, sin, net,
trash, hail, loll, loss, spas, sloe, erg,
glance, eel, leant, taco, orb, beg, grass,
shows, scent, tad, doe, eyes, set, tun,
newer, rare

## PUZZLE 35

The identical vases are: middle vase,
top row – middle vase, third row – end
vase, bottom row

## PUZZLE 36

1 (3) Trout 2 (1) Orion 3 (2) Tense

## PUZZLE 37

| D | E | B | T | S |   | E |   | F | R | O | Z | E |
| U |   | R |   | P | I | X | I | E |   | X |   | Y |
| T | R | U | E | R |   | T |   | T | W | I | C | E |
| Y |   | S |   | E | L | O | P | E |   | D |   | G |
|   | S | Q | U | E | A | L |   | S | H | E | L | L |
| M |   | U |   | T |   | E | O |   | O |   |   | A |
| A | V | E | N | U | E |   | J | E | W | E | L | S |
| R |   | E |   | X |   | E |   | X |   | X |   | S |
| B | E | S | E | T |   | S | C | A | N | T | Y |   |
| L |   | H |   | H | E | A | T | S |   | R |   | O |
| I | M | A | G | O |   | V |   | P | L | U | C | K |
| N |   | K |   | R | E | E | V | E |   | D |   | A |
| G | L | E | A | N |   | R |   | N | E | E | D | Y |

## PUZZLE 38

ACROSS: 1 Isles 4 Majestic
11 Transfuse 12 Bower 13 Iced
14 Hooded 16 Ski 18 Pay 19 Pastry
22 Marl 24 Kendo 26 Greatcoat
27 Repartee 28 Swift
DOWN: 2 Stately 3 East 5 Amend
6 Embody 7 Tow 8 Cordiality 9 Strip
poker 10 Ludo 15 Opt 16 Seal off
17 Uproar 20 Segue 21 Reef 23 Stow
25 Nip

## PUZZLE 39

ACROSS: 1 Rock 3 Cabin 6 Bell
8 Victoria 10 Tennis 11 Flakes
12 Super 13 Satin 15 Instant 18 Stud
19 Acid 20 Admiral 23 Party 25 Lunch
26 Trials 28 Letter 29 Interest 31 Cube
32 Welsh 33 Wire
DOWN: 1 Reverse 2 Kit 3 Carol
4 Blanket 5 Notes 6 Banana 7 Lesson
9 Computer 11 Friday 13 Stalls
14 Triangle 16 Sum 17 Air 21 Initial
22 Whistle 23 Public 24 Turtle
26 Throw 27 Latch 30 Raw

## PUZZLE 40

Silhouette 1 is artefact f, and
silhouette 2 is artefact d

## PUZZLE 41

## PUZZLE 42

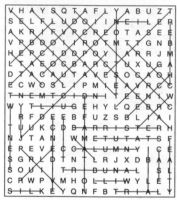

## PUZZLE 43

```
5 0 1 0 4   1   3   2 0 6 0 9
1   8   3   8 1 0 1 1   0   2
0   8   7   2   1   4   8   2
0   9   3 0 5   9   2   9   0
9 3 1 2 6   6 4 9   4 8 1 3 2
      9       8       3   8
8 0 0 1 7     5 9 2 1 6   0
0   6 1 2 0 0   3   5 1 0
3 9 1 1 3 6       5     2 8 6
  2       4 2 5 9 9 1   8
2 0 5 0 4   9 1 7   6 3 4 8 1
1   4   3 6 2   3       7
8 6 6 1 2   0   1   9 0 8 3 9
3     3 9 9   4 6 8       0
7 3 0 3 3   9 8 1   2 8 3 0 4
```

## PUZZLE 44

ACROSS: 6 Truncated 7 Elver 8 Din
9 Mode 10 Joss 12 Naturism
15 Biannual 17 Dispose of 18 Mitigate
20 Vibrancy 23 Chew 24 Chip 27 Ail
28 Annal 29 Piggy-bank
DOWN: 1 Streaming 2 Curved 3 Scorn
4 Studious 5 Oddness 11 Ironmongery
13 Twinset 14 Clef 16 Uneaten
17 Dams 19 Sylph-like 21 Ideology
22 Scrappy 25 Hangar 26 Satyr

## PUZZLE 45

ACROSS: 3 Sales 7 French 8 Over
9 Often 11 Baron 12 Critics 13 Only
15 Cup 16 Held 18 Trained 20 Appal
22 Noted 23 Made 24 Opened
DOWN: 1 Britain 2 Anybody 3 Shot
4 Later 5 Son 6 Pressed 10 Time
12 Could 13 Outcome 14 Lead
16 Happier 17 Learned 19 Enter
21 Idol 22 New
The character described is:
FRED PERRY

## PUZZLE 46

## PUZZLE 47

Artist 1 has an extra band on his sleeve. Artist 2 has an extra paint splash on his palette. Artist 3 has an extra button on his tunic pocket. Artist 4 has a tuft on his beret

## PUZZLE 48

1 (3) Grain 2 (1) Anger 3 (2) North

## PUZZLE 49

Picture 1 is missing a brick in the wall. Picture 2 is missing a carrot. Picture 3 is missing a potato in the top left box. Picture 4 is missing a banana. Picture 5 is missing part of the stall-holder's collar. Picture 6 is missing a wheel hub. Picture 7 is missing one of the doors on the van behind the stall. Picture 8 is missing a mark on the coconut in the bottom right box.

## PUZZLE 50

ACROSS: 6 Well-matched 8 Low 9 Wee 10 Wagtail 12 Idiot 13 David 14 Ply 16 Wonder 17 Archer 18 Oak 20 Awful 22 Moral 23 Typhoon 24 Ark 26 Ace 27 Dinner-dance
DOWN: 1 Pew 2 Float 3 Pastel 4 Acrid 5 Sew 6 Word for word 7 Deliverance 10 Woodcut 11 Latch on 14 Pro 15 Yak 19 Adhere 21 Lying 22 Molar 25 Kip 26 Act

## PUZZLE 51

## PUZZLE 52

## PUZZLE 53

ACROSS: 1: 258; 3: 213; 5: 112; 7: 32; 8: 199; 9: 361; 11: 345; 13: 815; 14: 56980; 16: 159162; 21: 110880; 22: 41760; 25: 211; 27: 110; 28: 221; 30: 270; 31: 51; 32: 900; 33: 441; 34: 295

DOWN: 1: 2268; 2: 834512; 4: 156; 5: 1939; 6: 1948; 9: 3791102; 10: 1568871; 12: 5040; 15: 6258; 17: 5916; 18: 110; 19: 1241; 20: 602112; 23: 1120; 24: 7070; 26: 1305; 29: 264
The date is: 29/1/1856 – the Victoria Cross was instituted

## PUZZLE 54

## PUZZLE 55

## PUZZLE 56

ACROSS: 1 Emit 5 Ogre 8 Aster
10 Manor 11 Brute 12 Ewe 14 Trot
17 Seat 19 Recital 20 Plea 21 Acre
22 Dialect 23 Lyre 25 Ever 28 Eat
30 Organ 32 Purse 33 Olive 34 Flow
35 Amen.

DOWN: 2 Mango 3 Tar 4 Stew 5 Orb
6 Route 7 Smut 9 Newt 12 Enclave
13 Entreat 15 Relay 16 Trade 17 Slate
18 Agree 23 Loop 24 Regal 26 Verse
27 Reef 29 Arid 31 Now 32 Pea

## PUZZLE 57

ACROSS: 1 Tripper 5 Halfwit 9 Refuse
collector 10 Worth 11 Elaborate
12 Reassured 14 Moist 15 Serve
16 Stressful 18 Nightgown 21 Merit
22 Ploughman's lunch 23 Test run
24 Tangent
DOWN: 1 Thrower 2 Infernal regions
3 Posthaste 4 Ruche 5 Hollander
6 Lie to 7 With a difference 8 Torrent
13 Roscommon 14 Musk melon
15 Sandpit 17 Latchet 19 Tiger
20 Nonet

## PUZZLE 58

Absalom, aBel, isRael, isAac, estHer,
noAh, ephraiM.
The staircase character is: ABRAHAM

## PUZZLE 59

## PUZZLE 60

ACROSS: 4 Ash 8 Full stop 9 Equate
10 Aplomb 11 Lead time 13 Edam
15 Moped 16 Debt 18 Black eye
20 Demons 22 Bureau 23 Encircle
24 Pod
DOWN: 1 Humped 2 Alto 3 Stub
4 Apple-pie bed 5 Herald 6 Rutted
7 Stem 12 Eat 13 Ebb 14 Mickey
15 Meet up 17 Bangle 19 Lout
20 Duck 21 Mark

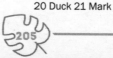

## PUZZLE 61

| C | U | B | I | C | L | E |   | G | L | O | B | E |
| A |   | A |   | O |   | X |   | U |   | V |   | K |
| R | E | S | I | N |   | O | B | S | C | E | N | E |
| T |   | I |   | V |   | D |   | H |   | R |   |   |
| W | A | S | T | E | F | U | L |   | F | L | O | E |
| H |   |   |   | Y |   | S |   | B | A | R |   | R |
| E | V | A | D | E | D |   | J | A | S | P | E | R |
| E |   | N |   | D |   | S |   | P |   |   |   | O |
| L | A | T | H |   | T | W | I | T | C | H | E | R |
|   |   | I |   | F |   | A |   | I |   | E |   | L |
| E | N | Q | U | I | R | Y |   | S | E | I | Z | E |
| L |   | U |   | N |   | E |   | M |   | R |   | S |
| K | N | E | A | D |   | D | E | S | I | S | T | S |

## PUZZLE 62

Cream, grOan, leaRn, riNse, spinE,
sTate: CORNET

## PUZZLE 63

The four objects appear in squares 3C,
6B, 7D and 6F

## PUZZLE 64

Beloved, deckchair, Roundhead,
difficult, tamper, rubber, rascal, lever,
raincoat, tantrum, muffler, ratio,
over, retina, aloof, flab, bus, Shrove,
eels, sea. The two diagonals are:
BUFFLEHEAD and CANVASBACK

## PUZZLE 65

ACROSS: 1 Share 4 Teacher 8 Dreaded
9 Strap 10 Later 11 Untried
12 Remedy 14 Obeyed 18 Central
20 Allow 22 Rated 23 Medical
24 Destroy 25 Ruled
DOWN: 1 Saddler 2 Alert 3 Endured
4 Tedium 5 Asset 6 Horrify 7 Rapid
13 Minutes 15 Boarder 16 Dawdled
17 Clumsy 18 Cured 19 Rider 21 Local
The person is: LOUIS BRAILLE

## PUZZLE 66

3, 5, 6 and 12

## PUZZLE 67

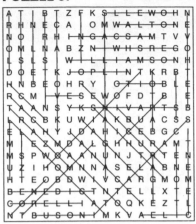

## PUZZLE 68

He WORKS with BOOKS and
PAMPHLETS, too, INTERPRETS
MEANINGS so that you
Can READ and UNDERSTAND what's
SAID
In LANGUAGES ALIVE and dead.
The person is a TRANSLATOR

## PUZZLE 69

## PUZZLE 70

ACROSS: 1 Information 7 Polar
8 Amidships 10 Rotting 11 Machete
12 Plain 13 Ancestral 16 Thermidor
18 Magog 19 Transit 22 Rat-a-tat
23 Committed 24 Adorn
25 Defenceless
DOWN: 1 Ill at ease 2 Foreign
3 Rearguard 4 Axiom 5 Insects
6 Naive 7 Peripatetic 9 Shed light on
14 Cartridge 15 Righteous 17 Mastiff
18 Methane 20 Aimed 21 Titan

## PUZZLE 71

```
1 2 3 4   5 6 7 8 9   8 6 4 9
3     5   7         3 7       8
5     6 2 1 2 7   6 2 6 2 1 6
7 0 2 7       7 8 2         3
    9 8 7 1   7       2 7 5 7
4 0 2     8 1 5 2 4   1       1
    4 5 6 7       5 0 4 3     1
3 2 2     9 0 0 0 9     4     4
    9 4 6 8 5       5 5 1 1 0 2
    2     7 0 1 4 0 2     6
    2     1     0       5 8 7 1
2 0 6 1 7     3 2 2 2 0       1
8     7 4 7 4 8   1   6 1 2 0
8     0         0 9   1       7
1 2 1 1   6 0 4 0 8   3 4 7 7
```

## PUZZLE 72

ACROSS: 1 Potato 5 Beadle 9 Often
10 Scruff 11 Glower 12 Reeled
15 Asleep 17 Yet 18 Erect 19 Die
20 Sip 22 Topic 24 Bee 26 Teacup
27 Donors 28 Pursue 30 Fringe
31 Lyric 32 Rotate 33 Redeem
DOWN: 1 Pastry 2 Turret 3 Toffee 4 Off
5 Beg 6 Enlist 7 Dawned 8 Europe
13 Eerie 14 Droop 15 Acrid 16 Eider
20 Stupor 21 Parrot 22 Tumult
23 Coerce 24 Bounce 25 Esteem
29 Eye 30 Fir

## PUZZLE 72 (continued)

ACROSS: 1 Clutch 5 Assail 9 Heart
10 Vermin 11 Talent 12 Rasher
15 Scouts 17 Tut 18 Larch 19 Eat
20 Set 22 Fever 24 Old 26 Prison
27 Waiter 28 Rascal 30 Pigeon
31 Given 32 Tilted 33 Teased
DOWN: 1 Covert 2 Unrest 3 Chisel
4 Hen 5 Art 6 Starch 7 Avenue
8 Latest 13 Auger 14 Raven 15 Screw
16 Table 20 Spirit 21 Tinsel 22 Forage
23 Ravine 24 Others 25 Droned 29 Lid
30 Pet

## PUZZLE 73

| J | U | D | O |   | S | C | R | I | B | B | L | E |
|---|---|---|---|---|---|---|---|---|---|---|---|---|
| A |   | U |   | V |   | A |   | N |   | E |   | E |
| U | N | K | N | O | W | N |   | S | I | S | A | L |
| N |   | E |   | L |   | D |   | U |   | E |   | S |
| D | I | S | Q | U | A | L | I | F | I | E | D |   |
| I |   |   |   | P |   | E |   | F |   | C |   | O |
| C | O | M | E | T | S |   | Z | E | P | H | Y | R |
| E |   | O |   | U |   | W |   | R |   |   |   | D |
|   | I | N | T | O | X | I | C | A | T | I | O | N |
| I |   | G |   | U |   | T |   | B |   | D |   | A |
| B | A | R | K | S |   | H | A | L | C | Y | O | N |
| I |   | E |   | L |   | I |   | E |   | L |   | C |
| S | P | L | A | Y | I | N | G |   | G | L | U | E |

## PUZZLE 74

ACROSS: 1 Insomniac 9 Obesity 10 Ion
11 Run in 12 On ice 14 Chute 16 Baton
18 Yap 19 Sot 21 Payer 22 Ovate
23 Vowel 25 Built 26 Hip 27 Article
28 Tormentor
DOWN: 1 Idiocy 2 Send up
3 Marketplace 4 Ignobly 5 Con
6 Reconnoitre 7 Midi 8 Type 13 Coot
15 Halo 17 Terrier 19 Sachet
20 Temper 23 Veal 24 With 25 Bet

## PUZZLE 75

ACROSS: 1 Quaint 5 Trance 9 Eerie
10 Ironed 11 Epping 12 Edible
15 Unseen 17 Roc 18 Exert 19 Die
20 Sow 22 Sleep 24 Shy 26 Prompt
27 Dilute 28 Rudder 30 Jackal
31 Rabat 32 Tandem 33 Meadow
DOWN: 1 Quiver 2 Atomic 3 Needle
4 Ted 5 Tie 6 Repent 7 Nailed 8 Engine
13 Donor 14 Exalt 15 Urged 16 Eight
20 Spirit 21 Wooden 22 Sphere
23 Pirate 24 Sucked 25 Yellow 29 Ram
30 Jam

## PUZZLE 76

LAPLACE

## PUZZLE 77

Weights A and C will rise, and weights
B and D will fall

## PUZZLE 78

THATCH

## PUZZLE 79

Sovereign, general, chieftain,
chancellor, chairman, dictator,
monarch, president, supremo, viceroy,
governor, captain, commander,
conductor, emperor

## PUZZLE 80

Pancake, yOghurt, taPioca, bisCuit,
rissOle, custaRd, chickeN
The other food is: POPCORN

## PUZZLE 81

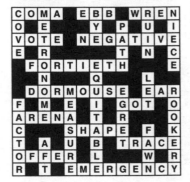

## PUZZLE 82

ACROSS: 1 Truncate 6 Musketeer 7 Lot
8 Cabal 9 Clueless 12 Undo 13 Beau
16 Self-worth 18 Car dealer 19 Iron
20 Acre 23 Neurotic 26 Visor 27 Bra
28 Nursemaid 29 Secluded
DOWN: 1 Timely 2 Unsettled
3 Clenched 4 Tremble 5 Oral
10 Southerner 11 Subsection 14 Enrol
15 Tweet 17 Largo 21 Chipboard
22 Doorbell 24 Upsurge 25 Banded
26 Vane

## PUZZLE 83

ACROSS: 4 Later 9 Achieve 10 Evict
11 Nan 12 Ram 13 Fad 14 Cremate
15 Department store 19 Linctus
20 Rug 21 Mac 22 See 23 Photo
24 Leak out 25 Nappy
DOWN: 1 Hatred 2 Sham 3 Perforation
4 Lend 5 Tin can 6 Reverse gear
7 Mikado 8 Stye 16 Pinion 17 Mess up
18 Excite 19 Lope 20 Rely 21 Moot

## PUZZLE 84

## PUZZLE 85

(grid)

## PUZZLE 86

ACROSS: 1 Orchestra 6 Weakened
10 Ski 11 Tease 12 Deposits
13 Disease 15 Band 17 Shoulder
19 Interest 21 Ring 23 Victory
24 Ignorant 27 Examined 30 Smashed
33 Hum 34 Era 35 Pressure
36 Enables 37 Clearly 39 Acid
40 Restore 44 Texture 47 Limb
48 Attempt 50 Exactly 51 Discover
52 Tar 53 Ire 54 Suspect 58 Resource
60 Sprinkle 62 Mermaid 63 Lend
65 Envelope 66 Ice-cream 68 Drug
70 Pulling 74 Doorbell 75 Ounce
76 Own 77 Recently 78 Greatness
DOWN: 1 October 2 Chain 3 Eyed
4 Taps 5 Asia 6 Widest 7 Approximately
8 Easel 9 Destroyed 14 Intense
16 Digits 18 Drown 20 Sun 22 Item
25 Ashamed 26 Temper 28 Instant
29 Earlier 30 Spear 31 Arabs
32 Descent 38 Letters 41 Edifice
42 Tobacco 43 Amateur 45 Untie
46 Egypt 48 Advertisement 49 Tories
55 Unknown 56 Peeled 57 Cain
58 Remainder 59 Serve 61 Pin
64 Degrees 65 Employ 67 Curve
69 Range 71 Long 72 Idle 73 Goat

## PUZZLE 87

ACROSS: 1 Walrus 5 Lamprey 8 Hyena
9 Pamper 10 Moth 12 Turf 13 Wasp
15 Goat 19 Flea 20 Caribou 23 Koala
24 Sty 25 Oxen 27 Cygnet 28 Armadillo
31 Bear 33 Owl 35 Eland 39 Gnat
40 Pig 41 Rat 42 Ewe 43 Polecat
DOWN: 1 Wapiti 2 Lemur 3 Shrew 4 Vet
5 Lamb 6 Met 7 Yacht 11 Hog 14 Seal
16 Aunt 17 Yak 18 Hound 20 Cattle
21 Raccoon 22 Polar bear 24 Steer
26 Elm 29 Amen 30 Slug 32 Rabbit
34 Hare 36 Apt 37 Doe 38 Ape

## PUZZLE 88

(grid)

## PUZZLE 89

F

## PUZZLE 90

RADIAL: 1 Resin 2 Ashen 3 Woden
4 Chews 5 Chant 6 Ceres 7 Cello
8 Plaza 9 Azure 10 Adder 11 Adler
12 Spear 13 Raise 14 Recap 15 Osier
16 Taper 17 Taste 18 Coast 19 Avast
20 Recto 21 Otter 22 Orate 23 Orbit
24 Drain
CIRCULAR: 4 Sward 8 Post 9 Err
16 Ropes 23 Terrace 25 Sow 26 Nell
27 Peer 28 SAS 29 Vote 30 Tee 31 Ire
32 Dear 33 Dual 34 Lei 35 Aspic
36 Act 37 Abash 38 Heir 39 Adze
40 East 41 Carton

## PUZZLE 91

ACROSS: 6 Sun 8 Environment 9 Rag
10 Direct 11 Semi 13 Pot 14 Doll
15 Final 18 Force 19 Love 20 Pop
23 Rate 24 Corner 26 Ski
28 Combination 29 Lie
DOWN: 1 Head 2 Overall 3 Brick 4 One
5 General 6 Strip 7 Negative 12 Pitch
14 Disposal 16 Costume 17 Council
21 Price 22 Royal 25 Ring 27 Oil

## PUZZLE 92

ACROSS: 1 Biopic 5 Catchy 9 One
11 Legroom 12 Rangers 13 Matt
15 Stamp 16 Garb 17 Nice 19 Downy
20 Lido 24 Surreal 25 Old hand
26 Emu 27 Hopper 28 See red
DOWN: 2 Ingot 3 Poop 4 Comptroller
5 Ceremonious 6 Tiny 7 Hyena
8 Plumpness 10 Ash blonde 14 Toe
16 Gel 18 Curio 21 Irate 22 Peep
23 Edge

## PUZZLE 93

ACROSS: 1 Coffee 5 Amused 9 Ivory
10 Carafe 11 Errand 12 Uneven
15 Façade 17 Sir 18 Lazed 19 Bed
20 *She* 22 Easel 24 Sip 26 Attend
27 Rascal 28 Knives 30 Oddity
31 Aisle 32 Desert 33 Draper
DOWN: 1 Cactus 2 Farmer 3 Eiffel
4 Eve 5 Are 6 Myriad 7 Scarab
8 Dodged 13 Night 14 Naiad 15 Fever
16 Delia 20 Sacked 21 Ethics
22 Endear 23 Ladder 24 Scrimp
25 Player 29 Sit 30 Old
ACROSS: 1 Scream 5 Yapped 9 Baker
10 Affray 11 Scales 12 Cherub
15 Benign 17 Her 18 Sugar 19 Dig
20 Boa 22 Sleep 24 TNT 26 Addict
27 Laxity 28 Mailed 30 Banana
31 Magic 32 Needed 33 Defeat
DOWN: 1 Starch 2 Rafter 3 Abacus
4 May 5 Yes 6 Archer 7 Pallid 8 Dosing
13 Herod 14 Built 15 Bagel 16 Giant
20 Batman 21 Admire 22 Scheme
23 Palace 24 Tirade 25 Tyrant 29 Dad
30 Bid

## PUZZLE 94

ACROSS: 1 T-bone 5 Toot 6 Valuer
7 Arch 8 Bunion 9 Bath cube
12 Aeroplane 15 Nag 16 On air
17 Ovule 18 Can 19 Every time
21 Man-eater 24 Untidy 25 Bran
26 Crayon 27 Once 28 State
DOWN: 2 Bravura 3 Nourish 4 Concise
5 Tranquil 9 Brainpower 10 Tyre
gauge 11 Year-on-year 13 Progeny
14 Anarchist 20 Renounce 21 Migrant
22 Attract 23 Endmost

## PUZZLE 95

| D |   |   | R | E | G | A | L |   | B | A | G |
|---|---|---|---|---|---|---|---|---|---|---|---|
| A | R | E | N | A |   |   |   | A |   | E |   |
| U |   | L |   | T |   | W | A | R | M | L | Y |
| B | A | L | D | E | R |   |   | G |   | I |   | O |
|   | F |   | A |   | E | C | T | O | D | E | R | M |
|   | A |   | S |   | D |   | E |   | O |   | E |
| A | R | C | H |   | D | I | A | T | O | M |   | N |
| D |   | A |   | E |   | S |   | R |
| V |   | B | L | E | N | D | E | R |   | T | E | A |
| E | E | L |   | A |   | R | O | S | E |   | B |
| R |   | E |   | S |   | U |   | T |   | N | I | L |
| S |   | D | E | C | R | Y |   |   | S |   | E |
| E | G | G |   | L |   | N |   | C | R | E | W |

## PUZZLE 96

| | B | | B | O | L | I | V | I | A | | R | |
|---|---|---|---|---|---|---|---|---|---|---|---|---|
| F | L | U | T | E | | A | | I | | P | R | E | S | S |
| O | | C | H | E | S | T | | S | K | E | I | N | | A |
| R | A | K | E | | P | E | C | A | N | | V | A | S | T |
| U | | L | A | I | R | | R | | E | D | A | M | | Y |
| M | E | E | T | | A | R | O | M | A | | L | E | E | R |
| | A | | R | | T | E | P | I | D | | R | | M |
| C | R | E | E | P | | I | | L | | S | Y | R | U | P |
| O | | Q | | R | I | N | G | L | E | T | | U | | R |
| B | R | U | T | E | | T | | I | | A | I | S | L | E |
| B | | E | | P | E | R | F | O | R | M | | H | | T |
| L | A | R | V | A | | O | | N | | M | A | I | Z | E |
| E | | R | | R | A | D | I | A | T | E | | N | | N |
| R | H | Y | M | E | | U | | I | | R | I | G | I | D |
| | O | | A | | S | C | A | R | F | | N | | C |
| H | E | R | D | | T | E | P | E | E | | F | R | E | E |
| A | | I | O | T | A | | S | | I | D | L | E | | V |
| B | O | N | N | | C | L | E | A | N | | A | L | T | O |
| I | | S | N | A | K | E | | S | T | A | T | E | | K |
| T | R | E | A | D | | S | | T | | S | E | N | S | E |
| | D | | D | I | S | M | I | S | S | | T | |

## PUZZLE 97

ACROSS: 1 Gregorian calendar
2 Remove; near; Nile; Aga 3 Ageless;
giant; fairy 4 Vend; rote; awe; rat; sew
5 Ended; read; lees; épée 6 Stone;
tan; scrap; raid 7 Osprey; dither; point
8 Attune; moral; orange 9 Preliminary;
mortal 10 Serene; send; raw; loll
11 Percentage; eclipse 12 Italic;
erect; orator 13 Tine; northern; Irish
14 Endanger; omen; stray 15 Fawn;
bedaub; bike; arm 16 Unison; gin;
elver; din 17 Leg; extend; reed; mess
DOWN: 1 Grave; soap; spiteful
2 Regent Street; inane 3 Emend; opt;
errand; wig 4 Golden rule; cleanse
5 Over; Dee; nine; inn; box 6 Resort;
Yemen; cogent 7 Instead; mister; edge
8 Aegean; ion; ear; train 9 Naiad;
strange; hound 10 Crawl; char;
December 11 Anne; ere; lyre; treble
12 Litre; aroma; connive 13 Elf; asp;
prowl; risked 14 Neater; oar; liar; term
15 Dais; pain; top; tirade 16 Agreeing;
also; saris 17 Ray; wed; teller; hymns

## PUZZLE 98

SIBERIA

## PUZZLE 99

Banana – 30p; Orange – 40p; Apple
– 50p; Pear – 60p

## PUZZLE 100

Pots, some, holt, gave
The phrase is: MOVE THE GOALPOSTS

## PUZZLE 101

| U | N | R | E | S | T |   | M | Y | S | E | L | F |
|---|---|---|---|---|---|---|---|---|---|---|---|---|
| N |   | E |   | P | I | Q | U | E |   | C |   | O |
| R | E | P | A | I | D |   | S | A | I | L | O | R |
| O |   | O |   | N | A | D | I | R |   | A |   | M |
| B | A | R | N |   | L | A | C |   | D | I | V | A |
| E | X | T | O | L |   | M |   | P | E | R | I | L |
|   | I |   | T | I | G |   | Z | A | P |   | C |   |
| M | O | P | E | D |   | J |   | T | O | N | A | L |
| A | M | I | D |   | S | A | C |   | T | O | R | E |
| D |   | E |   | T | H | R | O | W |   | V |   | N |
| C | O | R | N | E | A |   | B | O | X | I | N | G |
| A |   | C |   | S | K | I | R | L |   | C |   | T |
| P | L | E | N | T | Y |   | A | F | R | E | S | H |

## PUZZLE 102

ACROSS: 1 Howard 6 Ideal 7 Skilled
8 Event 10 One 12 Son 13 Next
14 Three 15 Court 16 Lord 17 Use
18 Man 19 Later 22 Domingo 23 Sales
24 Lovers.
DOWN: 1 Historical 2 Write 3 Died
4 Adventure 5 Plan 9 Tremendous
11 Centuries 12 Style 18 Monte
20 Also 21 Pool
The person described is:
ALEXANDRE DUMAS

## PUZZLE 103

1 Gos 2 Sip 3 Pro 4 Pel 5 Hon 6 Est
7 Per 8 Mit 9 Sen 10 Ate 11 Ten
12 Der

## PUZZLE 104

ACROSS: 1 Disrepair 9 Academy 10 Tip
11 Giant 12 Ridge 14 Corgi 16 Gusto
18 Hub 19 Arm 21 Humid 22 Igloo
23 Utter 25 Relet 26 Ass 27 Impasse
28 Directive
DOWN: 1 Detach 2 Superb 3 English
rose 4 Amalgam 5 Rat 6 Macrobiotic
7 Fend 8 Tyre 13 Giro 15 Oust
17 Saddler 19 Alkali 20 Mousse
23 Unit 24 Tops 25 Red

## PUZZLE 105

The words, in their correct order, are:
wHitelaw, Office, williaM, blunkEtt,
Straw, michaEl, jaCk, howaRd, hEld,
prioriTy, dAvid, oRder, countrY
The occupation is: HOME SECRETARY

## PUZZLE 106

## PUZZLE 107

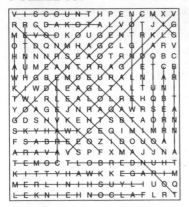

## PUZZLE 108

```
  9 7 2 9 2 6     4 3 1 6 2 9 9
9   6   0   5     2   3       5
2 3 3 6 5 4 0   1 3 6 2 3     3
5   0   7   2     1   5 4 6 0
7 3 4 0   3 7 6 4 1 8     1   3
1   1   2 0 9     8 4 2 0 7 7
7     6   5   8 0 3 3   6     3
  2 9 9 1 6 3       2   0
  5   6   2   5 4 0 1 0 1 2
4 3 1 7 0 1   7     9       9
1     6     4 1 8   9 3 2 8 4
9 1 1   6     2   3   5   0
3   1 4 6 6 4 0   3 9 2   1
8 7 3   3   2 6 5 0   2 5 7 5
2   2 0 2 2 3     8   1
```

## PUZZLE 109

1 Maiden, mined, dine 2 Signal, gains, sing 3 Admire, dream, mead 4 Garlic, Grail, liar 5 Orient, toner, rent 6 Repeat, Peter, peer 7 Formal, flora, oral 8 Anorak, Koran, rank 9 Rental, leant, late 10 Knight, night, nigh 11 Stereo, steer, rest 12 Convey, coney, cone 13 Seaman, manse, seam
The dancers are: ALICIA MARKOVA and MARGOT FONTEYN

## PUZZLE 110

Mickey Mouse, earth, Holland, dormouse, empress, Scotland, dentist, tarantula, Atlantic, Cenotaph, harangue, elementary, yellow, Wales, stiletto, orchard, duenna, aria, appear, recess, sangria, Arts, swig, garb, baa, alp
The two drinks are:
MINERAL WATER and SARSAPARILLA

## PUZZLE 111

ACROSS: 1 Go off 5 Tour 6 Gemini 7 Rows 8 Mature 9 Forelock 12 Limestone 15 Ear 16 Arena 17 Laird 18 Ash 19 Ridge tile 21 Sentence 24 Callow 25 Mini 26 Divide 27 Vile 28 Inert
DOWN: 2 Oregano 3 Failure 4 Bulwark 5 Tired out 9 False alarm 10 Remarried 11 Decathlete 13 Swaddle 14 Operation 20 Genocide 21 Solicit 22 Enliven 23 Chowder

## PUZZLE 112

| I | N | S | U | R | E |   | W | I | T | H | I | N |
| N |   | N |   | O |   | H |   |   | A |   |   | A |
| S |   | D |   | T | E | N | S | E |   | F |   | K |
| T | R | O | U | T |   | C |   | L |   | F |   | E |
| E |   | L |   | H |   | O |   | O | L | D |
| P | A | R | A | T | R | O | O | P | E | R |
|   | I |   | T |   | A |   | E |   | T | A | G |
| I | S | L | E |   | D | A | B |   | H |   | A |
|   | L |   | I |   | A | S | S |   |   |   | S |
| M | E | E | T |   | I | N | N |   | B |
| A |   | O |   | O |   | O | P |   | A | I | M |
| N |   | U |   | D | E | A | L | T |   | E |
|   | F | U | R | O | R | E |   | Y |   | H | I | T |

## PUZZLE 113

The antique dealer chose vase e

## PUZZLE 114

A cat was lying in a patch of sunlight and getting very hot. 'Why don't you move out of the sun if you're too hot?' asked his friend. 'Why should I?' replied the cat, 'I was here first.'

## PUZZLE 115

The Grand Old Duke of York, Humpty Dumpty, Old King Cole, Little Miss Muffet, Old Mother Hubbard, Georgie Porgie

## PUZZLE 116

ACROSS: 6 Temperament 8 Bow 9 Yam 10 Sidearm 12 Scent 13 Taper 14 Wee 16 Stroke 17 Breath 18 Bob 20 Upper 22 Pouch 23 Rampart 24 Asp 26 Pub 27 Taxidermist
DOWN: 1 Yew 2 Split 3 Frieze 4 Smart 5 Any 6 Touch-typist 7 Talent scout 10 Snooker 11 Matelot 14 Web 15 Ebb 19 Osprey 21 Rabid 22 Prime 25 Pat 26 Psi

## PUZZLE 117

## PUZZLE 118

## PUZZLE 119

ACROSS: 1 Dark glasses 7 Demon bowler 8 Pas 10 Sermon 12 Answered 13 Belief 14 Alarmist 17 Dreadful 18 Optima 19 Entr'acte 21 Gdansk 23 Ton 24 Hard-hearted 26 Omnipresent
DOWN: 1 Dam 2 Run to seed 3 Glow 4 All in all 5 Shrew 6 Supervision 7 Disobedient 9 Sidetracked 11 Rallentando 15 Repudiate 16 Butter up 20 Ashen 22 Shoe 25 Tit

## PUZZLE 120

## PUZZLE 121

ACROSS: 5 Athletic 7 Lie 8 Medal 9 Escapade 11 Exam 12 Anti 14 Cakes 15 Sit 16 Heiress 20 Off 21 Basis 23 Tosh 24 Floe 26 Advocacy 28 Annoy 29 Lap 30 Aspirant
DOWN: 1 Falls 2 Sheepshank 3 Red meat 4 Misdiagnosis 6 Alleviate 10 De-ice 13 Ascribe 17 Effusiveness 18 Root-canal 19 Ashes 22 Salt cellar 25 Acrylic 27 Spate

## PUZZLE 122

| C | H | I | R | O | P | O | D | I | S | T |
| O |   | A |   | A |   | U |   |   |   | E |
| N |   | S | N | I | G | G | E | R |   | L |
| T | O | O |   | N | E | E |   | O | W | E |
| E |   | F | E | N |   | M | U | M |   | P |
| N | O | T | E |   |   |   | S | A | S | H |
| T |   | E | L | F |   | W | A | N |   | O |
| M | R | S |   | A | S | H |   | C | A | N |
| E |   | T | A | D | P | O | L | E |   | I |
| N |   | M |   | U |   | A |   |   |   | S |
| T | E | M | P | E | R | A | M | E | N | T |

## PUZZLE 123

ACROSS: 1 Recipe 4 Virgin 9 Tar
10 Sonic 11 Sit 12 Near 14 Ogre
16 Era 18 Dozen 19 Lager 21 Doe
24 Abed 25 Ante 28 Tip 30 Amend
31 Hod 32 Nursed 33 Censor
DOWN: 1 Retune 2 Car 3 Posh 5 Inch
6 Gas 7 Netted 8 Incur 13 Atone
15 Glean 16 End 17 Ale 20 Tartan
22 Owned 23 Feeder 26 Mace 27 Idle
29 Par 31 Has

## PUZZLE 124

1 Boundary 2 After, heat 3 Sword, rash
4 Invent, lot 5 Loose, oath 6 Heaven,
toe 7 Under, soft 8 Merge, show
9 Evidence.
We need another, or others, to satisfy
the cravings of our human hearts. We
need to love and be loved.
Basil Hume

## PUZZLE 125

TO AND FRO: Initial, lever, rebel, lid,
damsel, laces, say, yarn, Nile, emirs,
Seine, eon, net, tubes, sirens, self,
fibre, eaten, nape, energy, yot, tepid,
dreg, gag, gel, leaps, sent, toast, trod,
dwarf, fern, noon, nob, brae, emu,
USA, all, lei, inst, tapas, strop, pin, now,
wear, rot
DOWN AND UP: Iceberg, gas, salt,
Tolstoy, yes, Susan, nil, Latin, not, true,
era, aim, Monterey, yetis, sane, épée,
Eden, news, saws, span, normal, lanes,

snip, part, ton, nab, brad, Dee, Enid,
devil, lilt, tref, fop, pip, panel, leaf,
feeler, rems, siege, Eros, sort, tong,
garb, bribe

## PUZZLE 126

| P | I | C | K | L | E | D |   | W | A | F | E | R |
| U |   | H |   | I |   | E |   | E |   | A |   | Y |
| B | R | A | W | N |   | C | H | A | L | I | C | E |
| L |   | I |   | G |   | A |   | K |   | R |   |   |
| I | N | N | U | E | N | D | O |   | S | E | A | M |
| S |   |   | R |   | E |   | C |   | S |   |   | A |
| H | Y | B | R | I | D |   | V | O | R | T | E | X |
| E |   | R |   | E |   | C |   | N |   |   |   | I |
| R | O | U | T |   | M | A | R | J | O | R | A | M |
|   |   | S |   | J |   | M |   | U |   | A |   | I |
| E | S | Q | U | I | R | E |   | G | A | Z | E | S |
| W |   | U |   | L |   | R |   | A |   | O |   | E |
| E | V | E | N | T |   | A | L | L | U | R | E | D |

## PUZZLE 127

ACROSS: 1 Wig 8 Labyrinthine 9 Tea
11 Drawn 12 Engross 14 Dare
15 Packet 18 Welder 20 Acid 23 Leave
go 25 Unite 27 Two 28 Non-alcoholic
29 Hay
DOWN: 1 Water polo 2 Glad 3 Abrade
4 Grind 5 Sneer 6 Thug 7 Untold
10 Astronomy 13 New 16 Crayon
17 Tag 19 Edible 21 Couch 22 Duchy
24 Exam 26 Etch

## PUZZLE 128

ACROSS: 3 Thread 6 Ladder 7 Special
8 Transit 9 Arm 12 Art 13 Drug
14 Date 16 High 18 Star 19 Mud
20 Ear 22 Regular 23 Anemone
25 Leader 26 Spirit
DOWN: 1 Advantage 2 Bedside
3 Top 4 Record 5 Away 7 Structure
10 Marmalade 11 Seed 12 Ache
15 Trigger 17 Hammer 21 Snap 24 Nut

## PUZZLE 129

| C | H | A | R | A | B | A | N | C |   | T | E | A |
| I |   | L |   | R |   |   | H |   | U |   | U |
| R | O | T | A | T | E |   | B | I | L | L | E | T |
| C |   | M |   | I |   | S | A | L |   | I |   | H |
| U | R | A | L | S |   | C | A | L | Y | P | S | O |
| M |   | N | I | T |   | A |   |   | S |   | R |
| V |   |   | T | S | A | R | I | S | M |   | I |
| E |   | S |   |   | I |   | T | O | T |   | S |
| N | E | W | B | O | R | N |   | A | O | R | T | A |
| T |   | I |   | L | A | G |   | F |   | U |   | T |
| I | M | P | E | D | E |   | U | F | F | I | Z | I |
| N |   | E |   | E |   |   | E |   | S |   | O |
| G | A | D |   | R | O | U | N | D | S | M | A | N |

## PUZZLE 130

## PUZZLE 131

## PUZZLE 132

| S | K | E | T | C | H |   | M |   | T | U | B | A |
| E |   | R |   | O | A | F | I | S | H |   | A |
| Q | U | A | R | T | Z |   | L |   | A | S | P | S |
| U |   | A |   | Y |   | D | E | N | T |   | A |
| E | L | O | P | E |   | E |   | N |   | R |   | K |
| L |   | R |   | J | U | X | T | A | P | O | S | E |
|   | I |   | E |   | P |   | C |   | K |   |
| E | F | F | I | C | I | E | N | T |   | E |   | Z |
| D |   | I |   | T |   | L |   | S | E | D | G | E |
| G |   | C | A | S | T |   | B |   | A |   | A |
| E | V | E | N |   | R |   | A | E | R | I | A | L |
|   | O |   | T | R | U | S | T | Y |   | C |   | O |
| T | W | E | E |   | E |   | S | E | L | E | C | T |

## PUZZLE 133

ACROSS: 1: 271, 3: 127, 5: 144, 7: 82,
8: 618, 9: 721, 11: 401, 13: 168,
14: 72328, 16: 623427, 21: 292005,
22: 24256, 25: 929, 27: 328, 28: 120,
30: 312, 31: 64, 32: 790, 33: 103,
34: 441
DOWN: 1: 2781, 2: 189861, 4: 222,
5: 1143, 6: 4802, 9: 7733961,
10: 1728000, 12: 1872, 15: 2770,
17: 2525, 18: 412, 19: 8423,
20: 759444, 23: 4239, 24: 2810,
26: 9041,  29: 290
The date is: 15/3/1877 – the first
cricket Test Match between England
and Australia

## PUZZLE 134

215

# PUZZLE 135

ACROSS: 1 Transform 5 Backdrop 9 Ear 10 Ozone 11 Embalmer 12 Scapula 14 Golf 16 Salvager 18 Unionist 20 Skin 22 Estuary 23 Nonsense 26 Fossil 29 Mislaid 32 Egg 33 Teaching 34 Sheriff 35 Enthral 37 Oath 38 Nonagon 42 Subside 45 Kept 46 Ceramic 48 Obeying 49 Fabulous 50 Eon 51 Dreamer 55 Golden 57 Enraging 59 Scuffle 61 Ekes 63 Memorial 64 Resettle 66 Sofa 67 Message 71 Time bomb 72 Total 73 End 74 Strainer 75 Abstained
DOWN: 1 Troughs 2 Sees 3 Okra 4 Menu 5 Breast 6 Cobbles 7 Delia 8 Portrayal 13 Chianti 15 Funnel 17 Glass 19 SOS 21 Kiwi 24 Naughty 25 Exeter 26 Frail 27 Schools 28 Ignited 29 Mason 30 Stern 31 Defence 36 Abscond 39 Oregano 40 Astound 41 Emperor 43 Idiom 44 Eager 46 Clown 47 Rescue 52 Raising 53 Angels 54 Ease 55 Gastritis 56 Louts 58 Née 60 Let-down 62 Stapled 63 Member 65 Enema 68 Soda 69 Alas 70 Etna

# PUZZLE 136

ACROSS: 1 Years 6 All 8 Escaped 9 Age 10 Men 12 Son 13 Panama 15 Sea 16 Add 18 Death 20 Lad 22 Era 24 Plight 26 His 28 Rue 30 Let 31 Running 32 Was 33 Owner
DOWN: 2 England 3 Set 4 Acts 5 Spanish 6 Admiral 7 Long 11 Had 14 Awe 17 Dealers 18 Dashing 19 Top 21 Achieve 23 Him 25 Crew 27 Sail 29 Ago
The person described is:
HENRY MORGAN

# PUZZLE 137

Tangles 1 and 3 will form a knot

# PUZZLE 138

ACROSS: 1 Countess 6 Musketeer 7 Lot 8 Soppy 9 Clarinet 12 Nude 13 Echo 16 Homeopath 18 Navigator 19 Idea 20 Ohms 23 Granular 26 Top-up 27 Boo 28 Scrubland 29 Engender
DOWN: 1 Comely 2 Unsettled 3 Treasury 4 Steepen 5 Prey 10 Toothbrush 11 Unthinking 14 Coast 15 Bough 17 Movie 21 Headboard 22 Culpable 24 Aspirin 25 Holder 26 Tusk

# PUZZLE 139

| | C | L | E | A | N | S | E | R | | T | O | W | E | R |
|---|---|---|---|---|---|---|---|---|---|---|---|---|---|---|
| M | O | A | | | U | | X | | | A | | | | I |
| A | R | M | P | I | T | | T | O | L | L | | R | | P |
| O | G | E | E | | | | O | | | C | R | E | E | P |
| | I | | T | | P | | R | E | | | | | L | L |
| C | | A | R | T | I | S | T | I | C | | B | Y | R | E |
| A | | L | O | R | E | | | H | | | L | | | D |
| C | E | L | L | A | R | | A | P | O | L | O | G | Y | |
| T | U | | D | | F | L | O | | | O | B | O | E | S |
| U | R | | E | R | A | T | O | | | A | | A | S | H |
| S | H | E | A | R | | | T | O | R | | F | I | T | | Y |

# PUZZLE 140

ACROSS: 1 Over the Moon 9 Bolt 10 Inclination 11 Left 14 Fibre 17 Manse 18 Totem 19 Vouch 20 Nurse 21 Eaten 22 Rotor 25 Mead 29 Toffee-apple 30 Noel 31 Deerstalker
DOWN: 2 Vine 3 Rule 4 Hindi 5 Motor 6 Obol 7 Nonentity 8 Statement 12 Amendment 13 Entreated 14 Fever 15 Blunt 16 Ether 23 Offer 24 Overt 26 Dole 27 Opal 28 Blue

## PUZZLE 141

| S | T | A | R | T | ■ | S | A | B | R | E |
|---|---|---|---|---|---|---|---|---|---|---|
| A | ■ | S | U | I | C | I | D | E | ■ | N |
| U | P | P | E | R | ■ | T | O | A | S | T |
| C | U | E | ■ | E | R | E | ■ | S | E | E |
| E | R | N | E | ■ | H | ■ | S | T | A | R |
| ■ | S | ■ | W | H | I | T | E | ■ | S | ■ |
| P | U | C | E | ■ | N | ■ | T | H | I | N |
| O | I | L | ■ | F | O | B | ■ | O | D | E |
| S | T | A | L | E | ■ | R | U | L | E | R |
| E | ■ | S | I | A | M | E | S | E | ■ | V |
| R | I | S | E | R | ■ | W | A | S | T | E |

## PUZZLE 142

ACROSS: 7 Panted 8 Earner 9 End
10 Atom 11 Dote 12 Tar 14 Delta
17 Gable 19 Credo 20 Sheet 22 Death
24 Add 26 Tier 28 Dome 29 Gun
30 Chaste 31 Girdle
DOWN: 1 Battle 2 Item 3 Adept
4 Cedar 5 Arid 6 Lentil 13 Amend
15 Lee 16 Act 17 God 18 Bra
21 Height 23 Temple 24 Angel
25 Dingo 27 Rose 28 Dare

## PUZZLE 143

| 3 | 2 | ■ | ■ | 4 | ■ | 2 | ■ | ■ | 1 | 6 |
|---|---|---|---|---|---|---|---|---|---|---|
| 3 | 2 | 9 | 6 | 4 | ■ | 6 | 2 | 1 | 1 | 8 |
| ■ | 2 | ■ | ■ | 4 | 8 | 4 | ■ | 1 | ■ | ■ |
| 2 | 2 | 2 | ■ | ■ | 4 | ■ | ■ | 1 | 1 | 1 |
| 2 | ■ | 4 | 9 | 3 | 7 | 2 | 8 | 4 | ■ | 1 |
| 8 | ■ | 1 | 6 | 4 | 1 | 9 | 1 | 8 | ■ | 3 |
| 0 | ■ | 2 | 4 | 6 | 8 | 6 | 4 | 2 | ■ | 2 |
| 1 | 2 | 1 | ■ | ■ | 2 | ■ | ■ | 5 | 1 | 2 |
| ■ | 6 | ■ | ■ | 1 | 3 | 2 | ■ | ■ | 9 | ■ |
| 1 | 6 | 0 | 0 | 0 | ■ | 5 | 6 | 1 | 3 | 2 |
| 2 | 2 | ■ | ■ | 1 | ■ | 6 | ■ | ■ | 6 | 6 |

The date in the shaded line is
16/4/1918 – the birth date of Spike
Milligan

## PUZZLE 144

Deck, Buoyage, Anchor, Funnel,
Freight, Ensign, Galley, Mainsail,
Riptide, Undertow, Lifebelt, Tiller,
Watermark, Marina, Gangway, Ballast,
Crow's nest, Helm

## PUZZLE 145

ACROSS: 1 Back-number 8 Elaine
9 Shanty town 10 Detach 11 Last in
line 12 Retain 13 Cape 15 Agitato
19 Adamant 21 Owen 22 Piping
25 Earthquake 27 Aslant 28 Humidifier
29 Tirade 30 Referendum
DOWN: 1 Basilica 2 Classy 3 Nutria
4 Metal 5 Rendered 6 Factotum
7 Inaction 13 Cow 14 Pan 16 Gainsaid
17 Trimaran 18 Together 20 Telegram
23 Squire 24 Varied 26 Thine

## PUZZLE 146

1 Charles 2 Edward 3 Bernard 4 Daniel
5 Arthur

## PUZZLE 147

## PUZZLE 148

ACROSS: 4 Logic 9 Agilely 10 Overt
11 Run 12 Oaf 13 Foe 14 Implied
15 French polishing 19 Capital 20 Cot
21 Pal 22 Ago 23 Panto 24 Knocker
25 Niece
DOWN: 1 Lay off 2 Riff 3 Deification
4 Lyre 5 Genial 6 Composition
7 Gemini 8 Stud 16 Expand 17 Palace
18 Galore 19 Cope 20 Coke 21 Pike

## PUZZLE 149

1B, 2C and 3A

## PUZZLE 150

Bend, Noel, seal, dart
The answer is: ABSENTEE LANDLORD

## PUZZLE 151

| P | L | A | S | T | E | R | E | R |   | B | Y | E |
|---|---|---|---|---|---|---|---|---|---|---|---|---|
| I |   | F |   | R |   | E |   | A |   | L |   | T |
| Q | U | O | T | A |   | A | Z | I | M | U | T | H |
| U |   | O |   | N |   | P |   | L |   | S |   | E |
| A | N | T | I | Q | U | E | S |   | C | H | A | R |
| N |   |   | U |   | D |   | G |   | E |   |   |   |
| T | U | R | N | I | P |   | B | O | A | R | D | S |
|   | E |   | L |   | B |   | L |   |   |   |   | Y |
| J | I | L | T |   | W | O | N | D | R | O | U | S |
| E |   | A |   | W |   | W |   | F |   | V |   | T |
| A | N | X | I | E | T | Y |   | I | M | A | G | E |
| N |   | E |   | A |   | E |   | S |   | T |   | M |
| S | A | D |   | K | E | R | C | H | I | E | F | S |

## PUZZLE 152

Plush, spaIn, Squid, hearT, cOast, Lover
The word is: PISTOL

## PUZZLE 153

No 6

## PUZZLE 154

Christmas, sedentary, yield, diagram, Martina, awash, happening, goddess, stride, exquisite, easier, rigid, double, elusive, error, ruler, roar, rota, arm
The two colours are:
CHARTREUSE and AQUAMARINE

## PUZZLE 155

1 Ban 2 Tam 3 Cor 4 Ner 5 Per 6 Son
7 Set 8 Tee 9 Hor 10 Net 11 Ter 12 Ror

## PUZZLE 156

No 3 with side b at the top

## PUZZLE 157

ACROSS: 7 Interest 8 Aged 9 Refuse
10 Astute 11 Star 12 Tendency
14 Academic 18 Also 20 Proved
22 Upturn 23 Year 24 Splendid
DOWN: 1 Intent 2 Required 3 Repeat
4 Attain 5 Wait 6 Hectic 13 Exacting
15 Career 16 Modest 17 Couple
19 Strain 21 Very
The famous person described is:
TREVOR HOWARD

## PUZZLE 158

The one in the lower right-hand corner

## PUZZLE 159

The unscrambled words are: arTist's, pArlour, painTing, Types, wOrd, dOlphin, skIn, deSign and selecT
The occupation is: TATTOOIST

## PUZZLE 160

## PUZZLE 161

| 8 | 1 | 2 | 9 |   | 7 | 9 | 9 | 4 | 3 |   | 3 | 7 | 4 | 5 |
|---|---|---|---|---|---|---|---|---|---|---|---|---|---|---|
| 0 |   | 3 |   | 9 |   |   |   | 3 | 3 |   |   |   | 9 |   |
| 3 |   | 4 | 1 | 1 | 7 | 3 |   | 3 | 7 | 1 | 9 | 7 | 2 |   |
| 7 | 8 | 3 | 0 |   |   | 9 | 0 | 5 |   |   | 8 |   |   |   |
|   | 7 | 0 | 8 | 4 |   | 2 |   |   | 5 | 6 | 2 | 3 |   |   |
| 3 | 7 | 8 |   | 7 | 7 | 8 | 0 | 6 |   | 1 |   | 5 |   |   |
|   | 2 | 3 | 6 | 3 |   |   | 1 | 1 | 1 | 2 |   | 6 |   |   |
| 7 | 3 | 2 |   | 2 | 8 | 3 | 5 | 5 |   | 8 |   | 7 |   |   |
| 8 | 4 | 7 | 3 | 1 |   | 5 | 9 | 7 | 8 | 2 | 6 |   |   |   |
| 3 |   | 7 | 1 | 7 | 7 | 5 |   | 1 |   |   |   |   |   |   |
| 8 |   | 3 |   | 2 |   |   | 6 | 4 | 4 | 2 |   |   |   |   |
| 4 | 0 | 2 | 9 | 8 |   | 4 | 2 | 7 | 9 | 8 |   | 3 |   |   |
| 7 |   | 3 | 9 | 0 | 0 | 5 |   | 1 |   | 9 | 8 | 9 | 3 |   |
| 8 |   | 2 |   |   | 2 |   | 1 |   | 1 |   |   | 3 |   |   |
| 8 | 3 | 8 | 7 |   | 8 | 9 | 0 | 3 | 3 |   | 7 | 7 | 2 | 3 |

## PUZZLE 162

| P | A | R | O | D | Y | I | N | G |   | S | E | W |
|---|---|---|---|---|---|---|---|---|---|---|---|---|
| E |   | E |   | E |   | N |   | A |   | O |   | A |
| R | E | L | A | X |   | S | I | Z | Z | L | E | S |
| K |   | I |   | T |   | T |   | E |   | V |   | T |
| I | N | C | U | R | R | E | D |   | K | I | T | E |
| N |   | O |   | P |   | F |   | N |   |   |   |   |
| G | Y | P | S | U | M |   | J | I | N | G | L | E |
|   | A |   | S |   | B |   | E |   |   |   |   | L |
| L | U | R | K |   | L | A | C | R | O | S | S | E |
| U |   | Q |   | H |   | T |   | C |   | L |   | C |
| N | O | U | R | I | S | H |   | E | N | A | C | T |
| G |   | E |   | S |   | E |   | S |   | S |   | E |
| E | F | T |   | S | C | R | A | T | C | H | E | D |

## PUZZLE 163

2D and 4B

## PUZZLE 164

No 6

## PUZZLE 165

ACROSS: 4 Web 8 Splutter 9 Evince
10 Crop up 11 Navigate 13 Tsar
15 Other 16 Dome 18 Maharaja
20 Caving 22 Lineal 23 Enfeeble
24 End
DOWN: 1 Spires 2 Gulp 3 Stop
4 Wrong-headed 5 Beaver 6 Hinged
7 Scut 12 Ewe 13 Tom 14 Roamer
15 Oracle 17 Mantle 19 Arid 20 Café
21 Veer

## PUZZLE 166

## PUZZLE 167

ACROSS: 1 Joker 4 Cabaret 8 Clipper
9 Apple 10 Piece 11 Freesia 13 Tree
15 Toffee 17 Shield 20 Note
22 Penalty 24 Ridge 26 Actor
27 Tetanus 28 Nuclear 29 Cheer
DOWN: 1 Jackpot 2 Knife 3 Replete
4 Carafe 5 Brave 6 Riposte 7 Theta
12 Rest 14 Rent 16 Fanatic 18 Heretic
19 Dresser 21 Oyster 22 Plain
23 Large 25 Dance

## PUZZLE 168

ACROSS: 1 Swinish 7 Easel 8 Pit
9 Last 10 Grog 12 Spectate
14 Outfitter 15 Asteroid 18 Calabash
21 Tradename 23 Operable 25 Ibis
26 Crag 28 Hot 29 Koran 30 Adipose
DOWN: 2 Wasps nest 3 Null
4 Superstitious 5 Seclusion 6 Stagy
11 Strive 13 Erode 16 Self-appointed
17 Acute 19 Bleary 20 Jet engine
22 Ambergris 24 Pithy 27 Skip

## PUZZLE 169

ACROSS: 1 Prevarication 9 Smarmy
10 Black ice 11 Maxi 12 Bingo
13 Pawn 14 Oil 15 Sue 16 Wren
18 Imply 20 Nick 22 Subtitle
24 Plasma 25 Introspection
DOWN: 2 Rumba 3 Version 4 Ray
5 Cabin 6 Tea cosy 7 Oak 8 Scow
12 Blister 13 Pennant 17 Roue
19 Press 21 Cameo 23 Tan 24 Pie

## PUZZLE 170

This person MEASURES you with a
TAPE.
ADJUSTS the DUMMY to your SHAPE
And WORKS away with PLEAT and DART
To make a FASHION GARMENT smart.
The occupation is: DRESSMAKER

## PUZZLE 171

1(3) Mouse; 2 (1) Under; 3 (2) Error

## PUZZLE 172

```
A P A C E   A F A R     E
  I   O   S   R     B O X
  N   S P I T E F U L     I
  C   T   D   E       A I L
P H R A S E     A   N   E
E   E   E     W R E C K S
A N D   T A G   R   M
  U   L       R O T A
I N T E R V I E W   N A P
    G   I   C     G   A
  E L E V A T O R   E R R
  M   N       I       A
Q U A D R U P L E T     M
```

## PUZZLE 173

Francis, seldom, *Mayflower*, risotto, oasis, stretch, Homburg, gander, repentant, trouble, Excalibur, radiator, rotunda, alike, enlist, toad, diverse
The two English ports are:
FOLKESTONE and SUNDERLAND

## PUZZLE 174

ACROSS: 3 Scruff 6 Tendon 7 Bladder
8 Patella 9 Ear 12 Gum 13 Pate
14 Limb 16 Bust 18 Iris 19 Gut 20 Toe
22 Eyelash 23 Humerus 25 Middle
26 Tissue
DOWN: 1 Anatomist 2 Dollops 3 Sol
4 Radial 5 Flea 7 Batteries 10 Rio
Grande 11 Abet 12 Gibe 15 Ascetic
17 Towers 21 Judi 24 Use

## PUZZLE 175

ACROSS: 1 Blackjack 6 Deposits 10 Eve
11 Exact 12 Producer 13 Scarlet
15 Zinc 17 Heritage 19 Analysis
21 Says 23 Assumed 24 Umbrella
27 Brighter 30 Sailors 33 Was 34 Toe
35 Examples 36 America 37 Theatre
39 Eats 40 Passage 44 Outside
47 Eggs 48 Pyjamas 50 Testing
51 Firewood 52 Use 53 Gin
54 Reached 58 Pressure 60 Deserted
62 Scratch 63 Dust 65 Material
66 Persuade 68 Echo 70 Release
74 Relative 75 Prowl 76 Lid
77 Solemnly 78 Yesterday
DOWN: 1 Breezes 2 Again 3 Kits 4 Asia
5 Keel 6 Depths 7 Procrastinate
8 Stunt 9 Surrender 14 Chamber
16 Casual 18 Admit 20 Ill 22 Area
25 Lowered 26 Absent 28 Happens
29 Elected 30 Stamp 31 Items
32 Stately 38 Rooster 41 Angrier
42 Sisters 43 Amounts 45 Irish
46 Edged 48 Pronunciation 49 Judged
55 Entries 56 Cuddle 57 Eros
58 Passports 59 Error 61 Era
64 Trolley 65 Merely 67 Scare
69 Chord 71 Lady 72 Asks 73 Epée

## PUZZLE 176

```
E X C A V A T E   K E E P
T   O   O   U   S   L   A
C A N A L   G R U F F L Y
H   J   U   G   B   I   M
  Q U I N T E S S E N C E
A   R   T   D   E       N
C H E W E D   S Q U I R T
R   E   R   U   N     S
I N T E R F E R E N C E
M   I   I   P   N   E   M
O R G A N Z A   T A N G O
N   E   G   I   L   S   S
Y A R N   G R E Y N E S S
```

## PUZZLE 177

Nos 4, 5 and 10

## PUZZLE 178

RADIAL: 1 Terse 2 Meant 3 Agent
4 Saint 5 Midas 6 Owers 7 Tsars
8 Harry 9 Diary 10 Abbey 11 Holey
12 Tress 13 Amass 14 Steep 15 Salts
16 Maple 17 Maker 18 Miser
19 Miami 20 Metre 21 Phare 22 Emits
23 Emmet 24 Sleet.
DOWN: 4 Tamest 5 Moth 11 Had
15 Spat 16 Err 19 Imps 25 Wing
26 Bias 27 Orme 28 Ale 29 Theme
30 Else 31 Die 32 Ear 33 Able 34 Plea
35 Task 36 Aim 37 Era 38 Arrest
39 Airmen 40 System

## PUZZLE 179

## PUZZLE 180

ACROSS: 1 Broken 5 Silent 9 Lines
10 Skylab 11 Cotton 12 Eleven
15 Lawman 17 Run 18 Donor 19 Bet
20 Sag 22 Serum 24 Cot 26 Traced
27 Seraph 28 Bongos 30 *Bolero*
31 Utter 32 Entity 33 Gyrate
DOWN: 1 Busker 2 Oxygen 3 Elated
4 Nib 5 Sec 6 Isobar 7 Entomb
8 Tenant 13 Lunar 14 Noted 15 Lotus
16 Aesop 20 Stable 21 Garnet 22 Set
out 23 Memory 24 Camera 25 Throne
29 Sty 30 Beg
ACROSS: 1 Reason 5 Obtain 9 Cedar
10 Reject 11 Remind 12 Skimps
15 Scores 17 Tun 18 Youth 19 Yet
20 Poe 22 Sieve 24 Sip 26 Island
27 Enamel 28 Anchor 30 Warden
31 Zones 32 Entrée 33 Bereft
DOWN: 1 Rarest 2 Adjoin 3 Occupy
4 Net 5 Oar 6 Breach 7 Apiary 8 Nudist
13 Kudos 14 Solid 15 Stove 16 Eerie
20 Pirate 21 Elicit 22 Snooze 23 Encase
24 Smudge 25 Planet 29 Roe 30 Web

## PUZZLE 181

## PUZZLE 182

ACROSS: 1 Bib 8 Enlightening 9 Rue 11 Prawn 12 Rat race 14 Tang 15 Papaya 18 Auntie 20 Nave 23 Lay odds 25 Essay 27 Out 28 Inefficiency 29 Oar
DOWN: 1 Bargepole 2 Beep 3 Floaty 4 Agent 5 Stern 6 Knot 7 Infant 10 Hereafter 13 Aga 16 Prying 17 And 19 Unsung 21 Astir 22 Eerie 24 Deft 26 Yo-yo

## PUZZLE 183

ACROSS: 5 Cohesion 7 Mac 8 Pasta 9 Reminder 11 Omit 12 Edit 14 Mug up 15 Err 16 Adverse 20 Arc 21 Tommy 23 Also 24 Anna 26 Envisage 28 Lance 29 Rum 30 Aspirant
DOWN: 1 Scamp 2 Thickening 3 Aseptic 4 Lopsidedness 6 Tax return 10 Worms 13 Aplenty 17 Decisiveness 18 Bagatelle 19 Byway 22 Managerial 25 Ascetic 27 Smith

## PUZZLE 184

## PUZZLE 185

Envelope – 10p; pen – £2.00; stamp – £3.00; tape – £1.00

## PUZZLE 186

Lath, goat, mine, rung. The phrase is: NO LAUGHING MATTER

## PUZZLE 187

## PUZZLE 188

ACROSS: 1 Senior service 9 Riffle 10 Incident 11 Stun 12 Bhaji 13 Cubs 14 Cur 15 Two 16 Zany 18 Inlay 20 Muff 22 Sit tight 24 Plug in 25 Complementary
DOWN: 2 Exist 3 Infancy 4 Rye 5 Erica 6 Vacuity 7 Cod 8 Knob 12 Bring up 13 Combust 17 Avid 19 Litre 21 Friar 23 Too 24 Pie

## PUZZLE 189

ACROSS: 5 His 7 Cambridge 8 India 9 Off 11 Serious 12 Late 13 Was 14 War 17 One 19 Else 21 Against 22 Two 23 Alone 27 Exploring 28 Not
DOWN: 1 School 2 OBE 3 Add 4 Beirut 5 Had 6 States 10 Grew 11 Set 15 Rank 16 Met 17 Obtain 18 Agreed 20 Enough 24 Out 25 Spy 26 Try
The person described is: KIM PHILBY

## PUZZLE 190

1 Pal 2 Let 3 Sul 4 Try 5 Hal 6 Ves 7 Len 8 Til 9 Hun 10 Ted 11 Led 12 Ger